HOW TO BE
TREMENDOUSLY TUNED
IN TO OPERA

Eric Oakley Parrott was born in 1924 in London, well within the sound of Bow Bells, and so is technically a Cockney but was brought up in Shoreham-by-Sea, Sussex, where he attended the local grammar school. After winning that school's most coveted academic award, the Gregory Taylor Scholarship, in 1939, he went to Brighton Technical College, where he studied for a BSc. in mathematics and geography. He then spent twenty years as a cartographer with the Hydrographic Department of the Ministry of Defence and, while there, edited the Admiralty List of Radio Signals. He began to write seriously in his spare time – articles, plays and entries for various literary competitions. He has always taken a keen interest in the theatre and was both an amateur actor and a producer, becoming an Associate of the Drama Board in 1961. He has had a number of his plays produced, and his radio plays have been performed by the BBC and in Germany, Canada, Australia and New Zealand, among other countries. In 1976 he resigned from the Civil Service and, after a year at Garnett College, Roehampton, taught English and general studies at Havering Technical College, Hornchurch, Essex. Here he compiled a number of units for the Longman General Studies Project. Failing eyesight forced him to retire from teaching, and he has now begun a third career as a full-time writer. His books include *The Penguin Book of Limericks*, *How to Become Ridiculously Well-Read in One Evening*, *Limerick Delight* (Puffin), *Imitations of Immortality*, *How to Become Absurdly Well-Informed About the Famous and the Infamous* and *The Dogsbody Papers*, all published by Penguin. He lives on a converted Dutch barge on London's Regent's Canal with his wife and son.

HOW TO BE
TREMENDOUSLY TUNED
IN TO OPERA

Compiled and Edited by
E. O. PARROTT

PENGUIN BOOKS

PENGUIN BOOKS

Published by the Penguin Group
Penguin Books Ltd, 27 Wrights Lane, London W8 5TZ, England
Viking Penguin, a division of Penguin Books USA Inc.
375 Hudson Street, New York, New York 10014, USA
Penguin Books Australia Ltd, Ringwood, Victoria, Australia
Penguin Books Canada Ltd, 2801 John Street, Markham, Ontario, Canada L3R 1B4
Penguin Books (NZ) Ltd, 182–190 Wairau Road, Auckland 10, New Zealand

Penguin Books Ltd, Registered Offices: Harmondsworth, Middlesex, England

First published by Viking 1989
Published in Penguin Books 1990
1 3 5 7 9 10 8 6 4 2

Printed in England by Clays Ltd, St Ives plc

For my grand-daughter Hannah in the hope that one day she will be inclined (and rich enough) to enjoy opera as much as I have.

Am I to understand that an overweight Italian singing in his own language is part of my heritage?

Terence Dicks, MP

TABLE OF CONTENTS

ACKNOWLEDGEMENTS

The verse 'Glyndebourne' by Stanley J. Sharpless in the style of Rudyard Kipling is an extended version of a Weekend Competition entry which first appeared in the *New Statesman*.

I would like to express my grateful thanks to –

Mrs Edna Smith for assistance with research;

Mrs Tricia Chamberlain for her care and attention in preparing the manuscript;

And finally, to my wife, Tricia, who has acted as my amanuensis for many years and without whose assistance at all stages, this book would never have reached the press.

E. O. P.

FOREWORD

I once saw a performance of *Fidelio* in which, when Pizarro was about to murder Florestan with his drawn sword, the Leonora, instead of drawing a pistol to protect her husband, could not, however much she jumped and wriggled, tug the pistol from its holster. As the trumpet announcing rescue sang out, Pizarro could have made a pin-cushion of Florestan for all she could have done about it.

At the world premiere of Delius's *Irmelin*, given by Sir Thomas Beecham at the New Theatre in Oxford, I heard the Princess Irmelin declare:

> These knights mean nothing to me.
> Some are young, some are old,
> Some are meek, some are bold
> But they all leave me cold.

That I had remembered these verses correctly was confirmed years later, when I read them in Neville Cardus's review, collected in an ancient *Bedside Guardian*.

Yet my pleasure in opera increases. Whatever the humour in it, or the humour it inspires in others, opera can take it. I warmly welcome, therefore, the parodies, neat and outrageous, in this entertaining collection which will add to the enjoyment of opera, and provide enjoyment in itself.

Jeremy Isaacs
Covent Garden, June 1989

PROLOGUE

A Song Against Opera

(*After G. K. Chesterton*)

After his Eden triumph,
When the Devil played his ace,
He wondered what he could do next
To irk the human race,
So he invented Opera,
With many a fiendish grin,
To mystify the lowbrows,
And take the highbrows in.

The recipe was simple:
Take murder, love and lust,
Add pent-up rage and jealousy,
And passion fit to bust,
Set the whole thing to music,
With words not said but sung –
(They must, to add confusion,
Be in a foreign tongue).

Hire costly prima donnas
And temperamental stars,
Big choruses and orchestras
With endless repertoires,
And you have entertainment,
(He rubbed his hands with glee),
Too dear for anybody
Without a subsidy.

The Devil has the best tunes,
So one can only grieve

He didn't give us more of them,
And less recitative,
In this most soporific
Of all performing arts;
Which operatic aria
Would ever top the charts?

The commoners of England,
They beg no maestro's pardon,
And do not give a tinker's cuss
What's on at Covent Garden;
Though deaf to Wagner's *Ring*,
They've learnt, somehow, to cope;
Opera that dare not speak its name
Is theirs – not Grand but Soap.

STANLEY J. SHARPLESS

The Matter of the
Plots

—— BÉLA BARTÓK ——

Duke Bluebeard's Castle

Bluebeard took Judith, a winsome blushing bride,
Back to his castle, and ushered her inside.
Seven grey portals, leading off the hall,
Seven grey portals, leading off the hall,
And if one grey portal should open in the wall,
There'll be six grey portals, leading off the hall.

The first door she opened quite took the maid aback —
A little torture chamber, complete with rope and rack.
Six grey portals, leading off the hall *etc.*

The next door she opened dismayed her when she saw
Halberds, swords and muskets, the instruments of war.
Five grey portals, leading off the hall *etc.*

The next door she opened on chests of gems and gold,
But not for her adornment; the stones were dull and cold.
Four grey portals, leading off the hall *etc.*

The next door she opened disclosed a garden green,
With walls so high around it, the sun was never seen.
Three grey portals, leading off the hall *etc.*

The next door she opened gave on a barren plain.
No human hand or voice enlivened Bluebeard's vast domain.
Two grey portals, leading off the hall *etc.*

The next door she opened unveiled a lake of tears.
Who could have wept so? Through O! how many years?
One grey portal, leading off the hall *etc.*

The last door she opened revealed his former wives
Who summoned her to join them in their ectoplasmic lives.
Now just Bluebeard, standing in the void,
Now just Bluebeard, standing in the void.
To what conclusion are all these signs deployed?
Don't ask me, mate, it's one for Dr Freud.

NOEL PETTY

LUDWIG VAN BEETHOVEN

Fidelio

(*To be intoned to the tune of the 'Ode to Joy' from the* 9th Symphony)

Beethoven, although prolific,
Didn't write much opera,
Only one, to be specific,
Still remaining popular.
Ludwig, being rather picky,
With a conscientious heart,
Wrote and rewrote every tricky
Orchestral and vocal part.

> Fidelio, or Leonore,
> Had not one overture, but four.

Here's the plot: a Spanish noble
By the name of Florestan,
Lies in jail after a squabble
With Pizarro, nasty man.
Pizarro, the prison head man,
Spreads the word that Florestan

6

Is a well and truly deadman,
While he festers in the can.

> Leonore, Fidelio,
> Florestan feels really low.

His wife, dressed as a fellow, quickly
Gets a job inside the jail,
Where a jailor's daughter thickly
Fancies her as though a male.
But she keeps her cool, believing
Florestan is still alive.
Faithful, to her purpose cleaving,
She will help him to survive.

> Fidelio, or Leonore,
> Truth and justice will restore.

Word came round that one, Fernando,
Minister of State and friend
Of Florestan would be on hand (Oh
Joy!) to bring his grief to end.
Pizarro, to save his bacon
Tries to kill poor Florestan,
But finds that he must firstly take on
Leonore, for her man.

> Leonore, Fidelio,
> A heroine! Bravissimo!

First the opera went badly
When produced (eighteen o five),
But rather than it dying sadly
Ludwig helped it to survive.
Acts condensed and score rewritten
Eighteen-fourteen, it appeared
Triumphant, as completely smitten
Audiences came and cheered.

> Fidelio, or Leonore,
> Ludwig Hi Fi Champ once more.

KATIE MALLETT

—— VINCENZO BELLINI ——

Norma

Young Norma, a priestess of Gaul,
Had hearkened to Love's secret call
From a Roman who'd said:
'Let's climb into bed,
Though your Druids won't like it at all.'

Pollione's power to arouse
Meant goodbye to her maidenly vows;
Two children she's had
By this soldier lad
Beneath all those mistletoe boughs.

Though she was the top Druid's daughter,
She'd forgotten what he had taught her;
Why Druids could do it,
But their girls must eschew it,
The opera don't say, though it oughter.

Her Dad (Oroveso by name)
Now kindles the Sacred Grove's flame;
It's a clarion call:
'Drive the Romans from Gaul!
Let's show them war's not a game!'

Pollione is tiring of Norma,
But doesn't quite like to inform her;
She guesses as much,
But still thrills to his touch
In bed, where his great feet would warm her.

It seems that he loves Adalgisa.
She's a priestess – it's rather a teaser!
A side-kick of Norma's
Who's suffering traumas
Whenever her wooer would squeeze her.

He has urged: 'Let us flee, me and you!
It is time that we sought pastures new.'
But she cannot decide,
So has not replied,
But asks Norma what she should do.

Adalgisa to Norma confesses
Shall the answers she'll give be all 'yesses'?
Norma weeps at the plan
When she sees the man –
This confirms all the worst of her guesses.

Adalgisa now has to know
Poor Norma's long story of woe;
Pollione's the clown
Who's let Norma down
So Adalgisa refuses to go;

But Norma still reels from the blow!
Shall she kill the children? Oh, no!
She'd really much rather
They went with their father –
Adalgisa must take them and go.

But she will remain vestal virgin,
Despite all her wooer's strong urgin'.
But soon he breaks in,
His lost love to win,
And indulge in sexual splurgin'.

But alas! For nothing is gained.
He's captured and very soon chained;
The stern Gallic law
Will give him what for,
For their Sacred Grove's been profaned.

It seems that these Laws require
That he be condemned to the fire;
Near yon sacred oak
He will go up in smoke
And the Druids start building the pyre.

Now Norma confesses her guilt.
(The funeral pyre is now built)
It is hers – the disgrace –
So she'll take his place.
And she runs to the fire at full tilt.

Pollione's now in a stew,
For he sees that her love was true,
And seeing his Norma
Getting warmer and warmer
He enlists as a fire-lighter too.

This story lacks humour, I fear;
Such views about sex, it is clear,
Held once down in Gaul
Might well appal
The disciples of Miss Germaine Greer.

E. O. PARROTT

ALBAN BERG

Lulu

Loves, husbands, suicides, and murderees
Undulate round this fascinating stripper.
Lay off your efforts to distinguish these –
Uppance comes finally from Jack the Ripper.

MARY HOLTBY

The opera concerns that evil which afflicts the over-sexed
    and over-rich . . .
Lulu, a whore, has married someone wealthy,
A doctor – rather old but fairly healthy –
Who's struck down by a fatal heart attack,
Brought on by finding Lulu on her back
Beneath an artist, whom she later marries.

This second matrimonial try miscarries
When hubby, in a fit of jealous rage,
Cuts his own throat – but, happily, off-stage.
Things don't work out with husband number three –
(She has this awful yearning to be free!)
And when the old guy finds her with his son,
She shoots the bastard with a handy gun.
When jailed for expediting his decease,
A lesbian Countess wangles her release.
In Paris, as a super-concubine,
It seems, at last, that things are going fine,
Until her pimp, determined to affront her,
Flogs her off cheaply to an Arab punter.
In order to escape from him she flees
To London, with three lovers, if you please!
The Countess and two males – but who does what
To whom and where, we're told . . . well, not a lot!
When cash flow problems call for a solution
She takes up her old trade of prostitution
And goes off with a client, Jack the Ripper . . .
It does not take him very long to kipper
The luckless Lulu and the Countess too.
Ring down the curtain! That, we think, will do!
It's not an evening full of light and laughter;
In fact, if entertainment's what you're after,
Or if, perhaps, you're easily upset,
The *other* Lulu's much the better bet!

T. L. McCARTHY

Wozzeck

Witless warrior begets
Offspring on unmarried lass;
Zealous, smart Drum-Major vets
Zones to which he owns no pass.
Enter penitence too late:
Cuckold slays his wretched mate,
Keeps a watery tryst with Fate.

MARY HOLTBY

A soldier's life's destroyed by poverty:
Wozzeck, 'a poor dumb ox', is doomed to be
A sort of guinea-pig for the higher ranks,
And does small extra jobs for little thanks.

Marie, who is the mother of his child,
Falls for a sergeant, driving Wozzeck wild.
His health is failing, reason slowly goes;
A diet of pulses aggravates his woes.
He kills Marie. The moon is up, dark red,
As are his knife and hands with blood he's shed.
Washing himself as in a trance, he's drowned.
His captain, passing, heard a funny sound,
But didn't worry – Levite-like passed by,
As rich men often do when poor men die.

Wozzeck said earlier, in a trifling quarrel:
'I'm far too poor to be content or moral,
But if poor devils get to Heaven – beware!
We'll forge some thunderbolts for you up there.'

O. BANFIELD

— HECTOR BERLIOZ —

The Trojans

If you think that you're in for a decade condensed,
And the whole of how Homer paints Trojan and Greek,
Then you're bound to be leaving the theatre incensed,
For the action is only in Troy for a week.

We open as Trojans, all trusting and cheery
(Except for Cassandra, who's properly glum),
Inspect what the Greeks have abandoned. It's eerie.
The end of the battle and bustle seems come.

Les Grecs (they are French in this case) *disparus*,
There is only the new wooden horse to assess.
Cassandra sees Hector, whose ghost passes through,
And she warns all the Trojans they're headed for mess.

Aeneas arrives with a prayer to the gods
Who've protected the Trojans through thick and through thin.
Aeneas himself seems the thickest of sods,
Since he can't see the terrible trouble they're in,

Not even when Laocöon has been eaten
By serpents for chucking a spear at the horse.
The fool still imagines the Greeks have been beaten,
And orders the nag into Troy. Well, of course,

This is barmy. Cassandra goes crazy with woe.
Aeneas, however, slips off for a kip,
Where he also sees Hector, who tells him he'll go
On a very long voyage. He sings of a ship,

Of a trip that will lead him to found a new city,
A worldbeating empire, a marvellous state.
A mate wakes him up with the news, pretty shitty,
That bloodthirsty Greeks are rampaging. So Fate

Takes a back seat. Aeneas goes out to defend it,
The Troy, thinks Cassandra, that's had all its chips.
We discover her urging the women to end it,
And to die with a *liberté* still on their lips.

Cassandra foretells, having lost her *fiancé*,
That it's Rome for Aeneas. Then each woman warbles
Complices de sa gloire. This is their final *pensé*.
Aeneas meanwhile rescues Troy's better baubles.

As the Greeks gape at women heaped up in selfslaughter,
They hear of Aeneas's flight with the loot.
He travels for mile upon mile across water
To Rome, though they're wrecked beside Carthage *en route*.

Here Dido, the Queen, is rejoicing in riches
Amassed in just seven years since they left Tyre.
She hopes for a hubby (a widow, she itches).
The Trojans are welcomed as dreadfully dire.

Intelligence tells of Numidian neighbours
Who intend to put Dido and co. to the sword.
Aeneas steps forward and offers their labours,
And Dido, who fancies this blade from abroad,

Accepts. The invaders are right-about-turned.
The next scene is passionate, set in a storm.
Aeneas proves all for which Dido has yearned
When they hide in cave which is snug as it's warm.

Now Love helps Aeneas forget that his mission
Is founding an empire, while Dido, in bliss,
Neglects all her duties, forgets her position.
It's a mess, it's amiss and because of a kiss.

The whole thing's a prequel of Cleo and Tony;
Aeneas should head for Italian coasts.
So Mercury tells him. Though Dido may moan, he
Must leave. So say several other old ghosts.

His *regrets inutiles*, he'll depart before dawn.
With Dido beside him, beside herself, raging,
He swears that he loves, but he's Destiny's pawn.
His love doesn't strike her as very engaging.

He leaves – oh! if only she'd burnt down his fleet!
She'll burn all the gifts from her Trojan *monsieur*!
She orders a pyre, her life is complete!
O Carthage! wails Dido, Carthage! *Adieu!*

Aeneas far distant, the court wears the tunic
Of miserable anger and hopeless despair.
Queen Dido predicts that a suitably Punic
Revenge will hit Rome – that an honourable heir

Known as Hannibal – he'll beat the Romans to pulp.
She stabs herself, suddenly seized by a vision:
No, Rome'll beat Carthage! She gives a last gulp,
And her folk sing Aeneas's name in derision.

That's it. Home is Rome for the young Trojan roamer,
And Dido has died on her nuptial bed.
It barely owes anything really to Homer,
Since Berlioz read up his Virgil instead.

BILL GREENWELL

— LEONARD BERNSTEIN —

Trouble in Tahiti

It is the age of smiling Ike,
Of range-style living and TV,
As Sam and Dinah breakfast like
The ideal couple they should be.

They listen to the jingle's tune;
They chew their munchy Toasted Oats;
They drink their juice, and pretty soon
They're both at one another's throats.

Then Dinah goes to see her shrink
(A must for all suburban wives).
A morning's work. A lunchtime drink
They cannot figure out their lives.

The afternoon means sport for Sam,
For Dinah visiting the stores.
It really doesn't mean a damn.
They live as though on separate shores.

But Dinah's seen a movie which,
Though trashy, has a point to state:
They're really poor at heart, the rich,
Because they can't communicate.

She cooks a dinner for her mate.
Together they hear 'Island Magic'.
They wonder how they can relate.
It's sad, all right, but it's not tragic.

                    BASIL RANSOME-DAVIES

— GEORGES ALEXANDRE — BIZET

Carmen

Cigarettes and cards eschew,
Amorous soldiers keep at bay,
Ranting bullprovokers shun;
Mind your manners: that's the way,
Even though you have no fun,
Not to get a knife in you.

MARY HOLTBY

This sad little story unfurls
With cigarette factory girls
(Of which Carmen's one)
Leaving work for some fun,
As they shake the day's ash from their curls.

It's obvious right from the start
That Carmen's a bit of a tart,
As, twirling her hips,
With a pout of her lips
She plays on a corporal's heart.

This soldier, José, a nice bloke,
Likes a quiet drink and a smoke.
With a girlfriend already
(Who thinks SHE's his steady).
He's happy enough, though quite broke.

But Carmen is like a red rag
To a bull with the boys. Though a slag,
She sets him alight,
Which causes a fight
With a toreador – what a drag!

But Carmen's as fickle as luck,
(Though José's affections are stuck).
When she cuts him off cold
He grows very bold
And stabs her and kills her. What pluck!

A moral comes out of this plot,
Though smoking is frowned on a lot,
When it comes to the fire
Of sexual desire
You'd be better off going to pot.

KATIE MALLETT

The Fair Maid of Perth

(*Mr William McGonagall visits the Opera*)

It was on the 26th of December, 1867, that the composer, Georges
   Bizet,
Who hadn't been to Scotland, even for a visit,
Produced his newest opera, for which the very excellent plot
Was stolen from our own great novelist, Sir Walter Scott.

In Paris people rushed to see *The Fair Maid of Perth*,
In which Catherine Glover, a maid of great beauty and worth,
Is courted by Smith, who makes her a brooch, and the Duke of
   Rothsay (a cad),
And also by Ralph, her father's apprentice, a devoted and lovelorn
   wee lad.

But the Duke's former mistress, called Mab, is a wild, handsome
   Gipsy,
Who has a heart of gold, and who doesn't get tipsy,
Unlike Ralph and the good people of Perth, confused and a-frassle
When the Duke takes Mab, but thinks she is Catherine, off to his
   castle.

On the stage I confess the whole story looks very silly,
With ladies in veils as disguise rushing round willy-nilly:
And it is no wonder to me that Catherine entirely loses her wits
When Ralph, and the Duke, and Smith plan to shoot each other to

17

But because it is St Valentine's Day the story does not end drearily,
Because Catherine is united to Smith, and the townspeople sing
   cheerily;
But I do not think that Bizet would have an opera one half so good
If he hadn't read Sir Walter Scott as we all should.

D. A. PRINCE

The Pearl Fishers

Zur-ga and Nad-ir are pearl-fish-ers. They live in Cey-lon. Zur-ga and Na-dir are friends. Zur-ga loves the priest-ess. Na-dir falls in love with the priest-ess too. They are not friends now. What will they do? Na-dir goes a-way. The vill-ag-ers need a new chief. Who will it be? The vill-ag-ers choose Zur-ga. He is chief now. Na-dir comes back. He is Zur-ga's friend a-gain. Here is Lei-la. She is the new priest-ess. Long a-go, she saved a man's life. The man gave her a gold chain. Here is Nour-a-bad. He is the high priest. Lei-la shows Nour-a-bad her gold chain. Now Na-dir loves Lei-la. Lei-la loves Na-dir. Na-dir em-brac-es Lei-la. Lei-la kiss-es Na-dir. It is not all-owed. She is a priest-ess. Priest-ess-es are not all-owed to fall in love. They are for-bid-den to get marr-ied. Nour-a-bad sees Lei-la em-brac-ing Na-dir. What will he do? He tells eve-ry-one. Na-dir and Lei-la are sen-tenced to death. Lei-la asks Zur-ga to let Na-dir off. Zur-ga says: 'No, I will not let Na-dir off.' Lei-la gives her gold chain to Zur-ga. She says: 'Give this to my Mum-my.' Zur-ga says: 'This was my gold chain. I gave it to a lit-tle girl, long a-go. She saved my life.' Zur-ga is the man Lei-la saved. Now Zur-ga will help Na-dir and Lei-la. He will help them to es-cape. How can he help them? He sets fire to the vil-lage! Nad-ir and Lei-la es-cape. Zur-ga is killed in the fire! Poor Zur-ga.

W. F. N. WATSON

JOHN BLOW

Venus and Adonis

Antefatto

This work that Blow wrote for King Charles II
Was first performed in 1684;
The first true English opera, it's reckoned,
Instead of Masques, after the Civil War.

Actress Moll Davis, Charles's mistress played
Venus; their daughter, (who was only nine)
The Lady Mary Tudor, made the grade
As Cupid; a no-Breeches Part, in fine.

Chorus of Olympian Gossips

'That trollop Venus, sprawling in the hay
All over young Adonis, *in full view*,
And snogging in her usual wanton way –
Of course, she's sex-mad – with a mortal, too!'

'That flimsy dress – you'd think she'd catch her death –
She might as well have nothing on at all;
And so low-cut, each time she takes a breath,
It's most indecent; she's not – you know – small.'

'*Now* look! She's pulled off every stitch, and there
Lies by him in the buff from tip to toe!
But wait! He's leaving – giving her the air!
(There *must* be something wrong with him, you
  know.)'

Epilogue

Alas, though, for Adonis, handsome nerd,
Who stomps off next day on a wild-boar chase,
For that's the gormless pastime he's preferred
To Venus's voluptuous embrace;

He's beaten by the boar – on points, I guess;
His groin, not Venus's, gets deeply drilled,
Which does for him. She weeps in wild distress –
Well – till by some new Love her cup is filled.

W. F. N. WATSON

ALEXANDER PORFIREVICH BORODIN

Prince Igor

To: Dear / My Dear / <u>My Dearest</u>:

Father / Mother / <u>Wife</u> / Brother / Sister / Son / Daughter: *(name)*

Yaroslavna

From: *(name and rank)*

(Prince) IGOR, General

I am: <u>well</u> / not well / sick / in hospital / <u>prisoner of war</u>

(if POW state holding authority)

Khan Konchak, GOC Polovtsians

Remarks / Message *(12 words only)*

Offer release if agree Polovtsian Peace Treaty: refused: Polovtsian dancers magnificent.

To: Dear / My Dear / <u>My Dearest</u>:

Father / <u>Mother</u> / Wife / Brother / Sister / Son / Daughter: *(name)*

Yaroslavna

From: *(name and rank)*

VLADIMIR: 2nd Lieut. s/o Gen. Prince IGOR.

I am: <u>well</u> / not well / sick / in hospital / <u>prisoner of war</u>

(if POW state holding authority)

Khan Konchak, GOC Polovtsians

Remarks / Message *(12 words only)*

Mum, you should see the Khan's daughter Konchakovna: really beautiful and sings lovely.

My darling Vladimir,

Dad's safely home at last after his escape. We trust you are well and will escape too though Dad says you are seeing a great deal of this Polovtsian girl. I hope you will not get too involved.

With love and kisses,

Mum

My dear Mum and Dad,

I am not a POW any more. The Khan has released me as I am going to marry Konchakovna and stay on here. I hope you don't mind.

Your loving son,

Vladimir

Honuord Pricne IgoR end Pircness YoRsaliva, Ples foregave me to meRRy youR sone which I luve vaRy mach.

Your luvign dughter-en-low

Konchakovna (*Mrs*)

W. F. N. WATSON

— BENJAMIN BRITTEN —

Albert Herring

You must wake and call me early, call me early, mother dear;
Tomorrow'll be the happiest time of all the glad New-year;
Of all the glad New-year, mother, the maddest merriest day;
For I'm to be King o' the May, mother, I'm to be King o' the May.

Old Lady Billows told Mr Mudd that Loxford's a bed of sin,
And not the kind of place to find a May Queen virgin in;
They kindly described me, mother dear, as 'pure as the new-mown hay';
So I'm to be King o' the May, mother, I'm to be King o' the May.

The prize of twenty-five pounds, mother, will go in my piggy bank
'A reward for virtue,' the Vicar said – I've your good training to thank.

There'll be dancing round the maypole to our favourite roundelay;
For I'm to be King o' the May, mother, I'm to be King o' the May.

There'll be lots of jellies and scrummy cakes and lashings of lemonade,
And I'll be the star attraction as I head the Grand Parade;
The people will come from miles around to hear the brass band play;
For I'm to be King o' the May, mother, I'm to be King o' the May.

*

If you wake, DON'T call me early, let me lie in, mother dear;
Today was quite the merriest time of all the glad New-year;
I got pissed as a puddin' and made a pass at Nancy across the way;
And if anyone asks me again next spring – I'll crown THEM King
    o' the May!

T. L. MCCARTHY

Billy Budd

Bid me to board a boat,
I wouldn't do it;
Life's hard and short afloat,
Land's nothing to it.
You do the decent thing,
But snakes accuse you;
Up-end them, still they sting;
Devoted boss must lose you,
Despite his grief you'll swing.

MARY HOLTBY

Hero – Budd, ingenuous youth,
    Cursed with painful stutter.
Villain – Claggart, foul uncouth,
    Bully, rogue, and nutter,
Pig-in-middle, Captain Vere,
    Plagued by sense of duty,

22

Situation – 'Ship of Fear',
    Far from home and beauty.

Claggart victimizes Budd,
    Incites the lad to treason.
He, poor soul, misunderstood,
    Tormented out of reason,
Struck Claggart lifeless on the spot –
    Copped a quick court-martial.
Delighted, Captain Vere was not –
    He'd hoped to stay impartial.

Come dawn, and Budd is duly topped,
A fate one wonders if he'd copped
Had all those in this sorry tale
Not been, without exception, male;
A woman's wiles, a touch of 'Soap'
And Bill might just have dodged the rope.

PHILIP A. NICHOLSON

The Burning Fiery Furnace

In Babylon, three captive Jews
At a feast, say: 'O King, we refuse
    To join in the gaiety,
    And worship your deity –
It's one of our basic taboos!'

The King says: 'How dashed indiscreet –
You shall die in a fire of great heat!'
    When he sees they're unhurt,
    He cries: 'Strewth – I'll convert!
Please send for a rabbi, *tout de suite*!'

RON RUBIN

Curlew River

There come som monkes on stayge who gladlye singe
And pleye their instruments lyke anything,
Then telle aboute a womman who is madde
Loude wailing for a sonn that she once hadde,
Which mayketh peple laughe alonge the weye
(As goode as Tom O'Connor any deye!)
But when they reche a river they muste crosse
The ferymanne she telleth of her losse.
Her sonn is dède, he sayeth (cheerful chappye!)
Which mayketh the olde batte moste unhappye.
But then she traveilleth to find his shryne
And heareth him, which dryeth her pypen eyne
And cureth her from madde, so she is gladde,
And al the monkes prayse God, which can't be badde.

KATIE MALLETT

Death in Venice

Cutting from Voce di Venezia (The Venice Voice) *1973*

REVIEW: *DEATH IN VENICE*
by Benjamin Britten
FROM OUR ALDEBURGH CORRESPONDENT

I attended the premiere of Sgr Britten's new opera for the interest the title appeared to hold out to our readers in Venice. Briefly, it is a parable of decay and death. An ageing and withered writer takes a holiday in Venice (as who would not?) to recover the springs of his life and art. He falls in love with a beautiful youth; builds a fantasy of remaining with him alone and hence does not warn the youth's mother of the danger of 'plague'; and then in the final act dies of this vague ailment himself.

I cannot believe that the Venetian Tourist Authority is going to be pleased with this opera, which uses Venice as a symbol of decay. Moreover, if Sgr Britten had applied to the Venetian Public

Health Authority, I am sure he could have been supplied with batteries of statistics refuting any suggestion that the city has an unduly high incidence of notifiable diseases.

It is important that these outdated stereotypes be exposed for what they are. Let Sgr Britten spend a fortnight next summer on the Lido di Jesolo to see the modern face of our beautiful region; let him recast his last act there and give the opera a more upbeat ending. Then, and only then, will I be able to recommend this work without reservation.

NOEL PETTY

A Midsummer Night's Dream

Tune: Widdicombe Fair

Hippolyta soon will Duke Theseus wed
All along, out along, down Athens way;
And four mixed-up lovers have to the woods fled,
With Nick Bottom, Francis Flute, Robin Starveling, Peter
        Quince, Tom Snout, Snug the joiner, and dozens
        of fairies and all, with dozens of fairies and all.

Fair Hermia has for Lysander long itched,
    All along etc.
But Pa says she'll be to Demetrius hitched.
    With Nick Bottom, etc.

To complicate matters and cause still more fuss,
Helena's mad about De-me-trius;

Titania and Oberon, Fairy Royal Pair,
About a Page squabble and part, nose in air,

At Oberon's word, Puck lets magic drops drip
In Titania's and Lysander's eyes as they kip,

Titania wakes doting on Bottom, who's grown
The head of a jackass instead of his own,

Lysander loves Helena now; she, poor chick,
Thinks that he's flaming well taking the mick,

25

Next, Hermia damns her for stealing her beau
And fishwifely compliments fly to and fro,

Till more Fairy Liquid resolves the impasse
And Titania rejects the embrace of her Ass,

All's well now; each ardent Athenian maid
Has the bridegroom she fancies by whom to get laid,

They all wed, but before they to bed haste away,
All along, out along, down Athens way,
They must sit through the tragical mirth of a play
By Nick Bottom, Francis Flute, Robin Starveling, Peter
        Quince, Tom Snout, Snug the joiner, and dozens of
        fairies and all, with dozens of fairies and all.

W. F. N. WATSON

Noye's Fludde

(With apologies to Joyce Grenfell)

Now then, children, I want you all to sit down and be very quiet, because I'm going to tell you the story of the opera we're doing at the end of term . . . yes, it is exciting, isn't it, Stanley, but we can be excited sitting down, can't we . . . George, don't do that. Because you are an opera singer now, and opera singers don't do that. And they don't rush about the stage pulling each other's hair, do they, Jane and Charlotte? . . . well, not very often, and certainly not when they are listening to someone telling them about the opera. Now, does anybody know what an opera is? Yes, that's right Emma, an opera is like a play, only all the words are sung instead of just spoken. Now this opera's very special because it was written to be performed in a church. I expect that's because it's about a bit of the Bible. Well, you see, it's about Noye and the Fludde . . . let's write it on the blackboard, shall we . . . well, Fludde is the old-fashioned spelling of Flood, and Noye is the old . . . that's right, Stanley . . . No, Emma they didn't call him that to *annoy* him, although I'm sure we all think you are very clever

to have thought up such a splendid joke ... yes, we do, George.
Well, first the audience sings a hymn, and then God ... Mr Hodges
is going to be God but he's busy today trying to find out who put
the plugs in all the washbasins and turned on the ... yes, I daresay
he *would* know if he *was* God, Stanley ... and Mr Wilkins will be
Noah, only he's busy today mending the windows around the play-
ground ... Well, God tells Noah that everyone has been so naughty
that ... well, breaking windows and flooding the washrooms, I
expect, Emma ... that He is sending a great Flood, yes, just like
ours, Stanley, only worse, and Noah must build an Ark. No, this
Ark is not an aircraft carrier Stanley ... well, this one *isn't* like
that. Anyway, some of you will play Noah's children, Shem, Ham
and Japhet, and their wives, helping him build the Ark. No, Stanley,
Noah hasn't got a power drill ... because he hasn't! And the rest
of you will be the animals that Noah takes with him into the Ark.
They all go in two by two, one little boy animal and one little girl
animal, of each kind ... because that's what God told Noah to do.
No, George, God didn't tell him why there had to be one of each
... because He didn't! Then Mrs Noah and her gossips make fun
of the Ark. Some of your Mummies will be the gossips ... no,
Stanley, not Mrs Wilkins. Your Mummy may say she's the biggest
gossip round here, but she'll be too busy selling sweeties to come
to rehearsal. Now, Mrs Noah refuses to go into the Ark, so Shem,
Ham and Japhet have to carry her in, and Noah and Mrs Noah
have a quarrel ... well, actually, I'm going to be Mrs Noah ...
no, George, of course they won't drop me, and they won't need a
fork lift truck, don't be silly. Or a crane, Stanley ... Then the audience sings another hymn, and the Flood comes, and all the gossips
are drowned. But it'll only be a pretend drowning, of course ...
because it will, George. Then the Ark sails on for forty days and
forty nights, and after that Noah sends the Raven flying off to
search for land, but the poor Raven never comes back ... George,
you can be the Raven, and we'll all have to look sorry when you
don't come back ... well, we'll have to *act* sorry, Stanley. And you
can be the Dove who comes back with an olive branch, which
means the Flood is over and they can all come out of the Ark ...
George, why are you hopping about? Do you want to ... No? Well,
sit down then and ... George, don't do that ...

E. O. PARROTT

Owen Wingrave

'Trumpet blow! Paramore shall welcome woe!'
The Wingraves' ballad's dismal phrases go.

Paramore's a gloomy country hall
With ancestors in oils from wall to wall.
The Wingraves are a military lot,
Heroes and generals with just one blot –
A craven coward back in Cromwell's days –
One who abjured his father's fighting ways.
Dad knocked him on the head to show who's boss;
He died, as kids will do, a tragic loss.
When Dad was sought to ring the funeral knell,
They found him in The Room, stark dead as well.

Owen's the last son of this noble line.
An ace at strategy, he looks set fine
For Sandhurst and the Guards, and studying hard
Till he comes out with theories by the yard.
His crammer, Coyle, notes to his perturbation
The pupil's pacifistic inclination,
But offers to break things gently to the aunt;
Miss Wingrave's stony and he finds he can't.

A house-party's arranged. The Coyles descend
With Lechmere, Owen's co-pupil and friend.
Dinner's uncomfortable – Grandad presides
(He is a general) – and all take sides.
Owen takes his tutor to the haunted room
And tells the reason for its feel of doom.

The general calls his grandson to his study
And disinherits him. The outcome will be bloody.
Kate, the fiancée, flirts with his best friend
And then provokes her lover to his end.
She calls him 'coward', dares him to a night
Locked in with the two ghosts. He says: 'All right.'
Kate sneaks to let him out in the small hours,
Then shrieks, awed by the supernatural powers.

Both guests and family flock to the door
And find young Owen dead upon the floor,
Slain by the military curse of Paramore.

FIONA PITT-KETHLEY

Peter Grimes

I must go down to the seas again, to the Aldeburgh seas with a boy,
And all I ask is an orphan lad, and the Pleiades on high.
Now the inquest done, and the storm's come, and Auntie's bar is
  shaking,
But the carrier's in 'mid the drunken din with a new lad ripe for
  breaking.

I must go down to the seas again, to escape from Sunday's throng,
From po-faced Mrs Sedley and the Rector's fluting song,
And Ellen's 'broidery that fails to stop her crying,
And the lad who died because he tried – like seagulls – flying.

I must go down to the seas again, for Balstrode says my boat
Should leave the Borough beaches, and then – forget to float.
They're a crabby lot these Aldeburgh souls to condemn a fellow-rover
To a fishy grave in the North Sea wave when the opera's over.

D. A. PRINCE

The Rape of Lucretia

Tarquinius Superbus, the ruler of Rome,
Was discussing with some of his men
Whether wives do or don't remain faithful at home
When their sires are campaigning again.
On a night when some unannounced visits were made
Only one wife – Lucretia – was not being laid.

To his charioteer he called: 'Full speed ahead!'
And made for Lucretia's house;
He was courteously offered a bite and a bed,
And he crept off as quiet as a mouse.
Overnight, the fair matron was raped at his hands,
And she killed herself later, as honour demands.

*

Queen Mary, at Glyndebourne, just after the show,
Demanded of Benjamin Britten:
'Why choose such a theme, that's what we want to
   know?'
Poor Ben with confusion was smitten.
And all he could hear was himself blabbering:
'Ma'am, I'm interested rather in that sort of thing.'

T. L. MCCARTHY

The Turn of the Screw

How doth the busy Governess
Improve her charges' work
Aware what sin they wallow in
Behind their prissy smirk;

For Flora dear and darling Miles
Both greet with guilty zest
The spooks of two departed crooks
By whom they are Possessed.

One is their lewd ex-governess
Miss Jessel, who in bed
Had Peter Quint do many a stint –
And now they're very dead.

Though these grim ghouls weave wicked wiles
The children to entrap,
Whenever Miss tells someone this,
They say: 'What utter crap!'

So she girds up her lissom loins,
And all alone must wrestle
For Miles and Flo to be let go
By Quint and vile Miss Jessel.

But stay! At last the Housekeeper,
Convinced, takes Flo away,
And Miss can face the spectral brace
To baulk them of their prey.

She strives for Miles's heart and soul,
And wins! She hasn't fluffed it!
She smiles – but in her arms dear Miles
Has been and gone and snuffed it.

So, children, spurn the urge to learn
What tickles peccant palate,
Nor try to guess what Governess
Gets up to with the Valet.

W. F. N. WATSON

ALFREDO CATALANI

La Wally

The opera's title *La Wally*
Suggests to us fun, farce, and folly,
And when at the end
She dives after her friend
Through an avalanche – *that* should be jolly.

MARY HOLTBY

LUIGI CHERUBINI

Médée

A FRAGMENT OF A GREEK PLAY

MÉDÉE, CHORUS.

MÉDÉE: O woeful day! What dire troubles
Inflict themselves upon me!

CHORUS LEADER: From your speech and girth
I judge you an operatic soprano.

CHORUS: With such tidings what else could she be?

MÉDÉE: You have spoken sooth.

CHORUS: And you will ere long relate your painful history
In a brief and poignant aria.

MÉDÉE: My tale is a long one.
Likewise my song.

CHORUS: You give voice to our secret dread.
Gather therefore your breath into your body-box
And get on with it.

MÉDÉE: Know then that my husband is Jason,
He who obtained the Golden Fleece
With my aid.

CHORUS: We know the tale.
Pray do not incommode yourself with its repetition.

MÉDÉE: We were wed according to the custom
Of the land of my nurture.

CHORUS: But not legally accepted in civilized countries.

MÉDÉE: We lived as man and wife.
I bore him two sons.

CHORUS: Had you not also bored him
He would not have hied him here to Corinth.

CHORUS LEADER: Bearing his sons with him.

MÉDÉE: You overleap my story.

CHORUS: We but rescue ourselves from tedium.

MÉDÉE: Know therefore that he has betrothed himself
to Glauce
King Creon's daughter.

CHORUS: Having renounced his vows to you
Who then arrived to see your children.

CHORUS LEADER: But also seeking a dreadful revenge
Instead of enjoying your new-found freedom
With good prospects of a career in witchcraft.

CHORUS: A liberated woman.

MÉDÉE: The Corinthians reviled me, demanding my
death
Or banishment.

CHORUS: We know just how they felt.

MÉDÉE: But Creon granted me one day
And I have sent jewels to Glauce
The bride of today.

CHORUS: Which, of course, were poisoned.

CHORUS LEADER: I heard her death cries earlier.

MÉDÉE: You seem to know everything.

CHORUS: We have but to stand here
And people disgorge to us their woes.

MÉDÉE: But you could not know
That I have just slain my children.

CHORUS: This we surmised from the bloody knife.
Did not we see you just now
Set fire to the marriage temple of Hero
And prepare to perish in its flames?

MÉDÉE: After singing my aria of suicide.

CHORUS: Before you are done, doubtless
We shall feel the same way.
Call no man happy who is forced
To listen to a lot of coloratura sopranos.

E. O. PARROTT

33

CLAUDE DEBUSSY

Pelléas and Mélisande

O, what can ail thee, knight at arms?
> Why wand'rest, Golaud, here at eve?
The audience have all gone home,
> Why do you grieve?

'I met a Maiden by the Spring,
> Like to a child of elfin lore;
Her beauteous name was Mélisande.
> I loved her, sure.

I led her off and married her,
> Then to my brother, Pelléas,
I sent a missive telling what
> Had come to pass.

From my old grandsire did he bring
> Pardon and love, full many a mile,
But when they met, my lovely bride
> Did him beguile.

So did he, her, though without fault
> Did their enchanted love remain
But to my suffering soul it brought
> Infinite pain.

He took her to a shaded spot
> Where she did sport beside a spring
And in the fountain's deeps there fell
> My love-gift ring.

And as the ring fell from her hand,
> By eldritch power my steed did rear
And injured me, so that I lay
> On sick bed drear.

And there I saw her ringless hand
> And in my awful agony

I sent her forth to seek the jewel
    Down by the sea.

So she and Pelléas sadly sought
    But found it not in that far place
Eftsoons he must depart from her
    With one embrace.

A chaste and brotherly embrace,
    But all her hair did o'er him flow,
And 'twas in tortured rage that I
    Did bid him go.

Then through the icy vaults of doom
    I led my brother by the hand,
Begging him, earnestly, to shun
    My Mélisande.

I held my son up in my arms
    To spy through casements on the twain,
But nought could he report to me.
    I feared in vain.

Then, though I knew her innocent,
    I seized my loved one by the hair;
I hurled her down upon the ground
    And left her there.

I found them, by the fountain side.
    I took my sword and struck him dead;
And when I turned and wounded her,
    Mélisande fled.

Then, even on her bed of death,
    I threatened her with questions wild,
Till she, at last, yielded the ghost,
    Holding her child.

And that is why I sojourn here
    Although the orchestra has left.
And usherettes have all gone home
    And I'm bereft.'

GERARD BENSON

—— FREDERICK DELIUS ——

A Village Romeo and Juliet

The story involves a Swiss mister and miss,
Called Sali and Vreli, who had
Their minds set on marriage; (they'd shared their first kiss
At play-school) but now things look bad!
Their fathers, both farmers, and once very rich,
Have ruined themselves and their heirs
By squabbling in court over border-land which
They both claim is rightfully theirs.

In most other countries (and that includes us)
Young folk, when they start going steady,
See little occasion to kick up a fuss
Should parents be strapped for the ready.
But the Swiss are a purse-proud and miserly bunch,
Obsessed with francs, dollars and pounds;
And if losses occur and it comes to the crunch,
They emit silly falsetto sounds.

What with Vreli's old father clean out of his mind
(A blow from young Sali did that)
And the rent on her old home a long way behind
(The bailiff's dropped in for a chat!)
The pair take the view that the pressures are such
As to merit a fling at the Fair,
But the bright lights and noise do not help overmuch
As they forthwith give way to despair.

Then the curtain comes down, as they gloomily stalk
Off the stage for their next escapade,
After which the well-known intermezzo, 'The Walk
To the Paradise Garden' is played;
And the next scene is set at a riverside inn
Where a party of vagabonds sit.

'Come and join us,' the Dark Fiddler shouts through the
   din.
(This the class structure does not permit!)

Tied up close by the inn, there's a barge full of hay –
The pair sneak aboard up the plank!
In a very few moments the craft's under way
And it drifts gently clear of the bank.
Yes, the hay's a fine place for a last kiss and hug;
Vreli tosses some flowers to the waves.
Sali goes to the hold and he pulls out the plug . . .
Down they go to their watery graves!

'The Walk to the Paradise Garden' – you what?
You expected the last scene to be
All alive with bright angels, saints, cherubs – the lot . . . ?
Well, to tell you the truth, so did we!
But the Walk's but a trek through a Swiss mountain pass –
(The librettist's been hellishly clever!)
And the Paradise Garden no more than, alas,
Just the name of that pub by the river!

T. L. MCCARTHY

—— GAETANO DONIZETTI ——

Anna Bolena

See King Hal, the Royal Satyr,
Never one for idle chatter,
Grimly letching for Jane Seymour's
Maiden charms and virgin femurs.

See Jane say: 'There lies herein
Sin: You're wed to Anne Boleyn',
(Who in operatic *scena*
We must call 'Anna Bolena').

See, to end their controversy,
Lord Northumberland (or Percy),
Ex-flame Anne might fancy laying –
Will she? Does she? There's no saying.

See King Hal with royal malice
Feigning fury round the palace,
While in secret he's exulting,
Bawling out the words insulting:

'Randy *lèse*-majestic strumpet,
Flogging Perce our Royal Crumpet';
See her sentenced to be led off
To the Tower to have her head off.

W. F. N. WATSON

The Daughter of the Regiment

(*To the tune of 'The British Grenadiers'*)

Some regiments have mascots,
Like dogs, or goats, or sheep,
But this one has a daughter,
Who lately earns her keep
By keeping men in victuals
And bringing them good cheer,
In all a good luck token
For a happy grenadier.

Adopted as a baby
Marie, who's now full grown,
Has found a foreign suitor
She wants to be her own.
But he must be a soldier
And so he joins the troop –
But then her mother finds her,
She's hardly cock-a-hoop!

Mum would prefer her daughter
Was married to a duke,
And so she's made arrangements,

(Though Marie just wants to puke).
But at the wedding party
The grenadiers protest
By bringing up her background,
To shock each noble guest.

The guests are quite astounded,
(This girl is quite Non-U),
Embarrassed and confounded
Her mother gives in too,
And lets her daughter marry
Her Tonio – her choice,
And all (Tom, Dick and Harry),
The grenadiers rejoice,

With a ra ra ra for their Daughter's ma!
And France, in lusty voice.

KATIE MALLETT

Don Pasquale

Donizetti's Don Pasquale
Is a bachelor, old and gnarly;
But, to spite his nephew, he
Wants to marry. Trustingly
He turns to Dr Malatesta,
Who is friendly, but a jester.
Whom does Malatesta find?
The girl the *nephew* has in mind,
A teenage widow called Norina!
What idea could be obscener
Than that such a lovely bride
To a dotard should be tied?

Ernesto is the nephew's name.
He cannot hope to wed his dame
Once he knows the Don's to marry.
'Alas!' he cries, 'I must not tarry;
I'm off abroad: for now, I see
There's no inheritance for me.'

39

Malatesta brings his 'sister' –
It's Norina! What a twister! –
Into Don Pasquale's house.
'Come, my pretty little mouse!'
Cries the Don, 'I'll be your votary.'
As it happens, there's a notary
Convenient to tie the knot
While the Don is fiery-hot.
No one doubts the fellow's fitness;
And Ernesto is a witness!
(Malatesta's told his plan
To that poor unhappy man.)

Once Norina is a wife,
She makes her so-called husband's life
A misery, won't let him pet her,
Insists his manners must be better,
Demands more furniture, a coach,
A host of servants, and a brooch;
Also a younger man – hey presto!
She wants the presence of Ernesto!

Quarrels follow, at a pace;
Norina even slaps his face;
Then right in front of Don Pasquale,
Though sad to make him such a charlie,
She drops a note, by way of mockery,
Calling a lover to the rockery.
He quickly summons Malatesta
And asks him if he can suggest a
Way by which he might outwit
The plottings of this little bit.

Now comes a wonderful duet
As Malatesta's trap is set:
He and Pasquale join to gloat
That each has someone by the throat:
Pasquale has his Amazon,
But Malatesta has the Don!

After a love scene in the garden
The Don demands she beg his pardon.

Norina promptly starts to scoff;
The match will have to be called off;
But Malatesta's main condition
Is that Pasquale's full permission
Is given for Ernesto's wish
To be united with his dish.
What dish is this? The very minx
Who's played this game of tiddlywinks.
Ernesto now is all Norina's:
The Don's been taken to the cleaners.

At first he nearly blows apart;
But he's a good old chap at heart:
His protests quickly turn to laughter,
And all live happily ever after.

PAUL GRIFFIN

L'elisir d'amore

Dear Lucia,

I am engaged to be married. Yes, I really am. To a terribly glamorous army sergeant called Belcore. (Such a wonderfully sexy uniform he has.) Of course, there is this poor peasant, Nemorino, who has a thing about me. But he is such a wet, apart from not having enough of the ready! The poor dope even bought a so-called love potion from some dreadful fairground quack called Dulcamara. It was only ghastly red plonk and just made him pissed so that he made a fool of himself in front of the entire village.

So glad to hear about you and Edgardo. What you tell me about what you did in the heather sounds real fun.

Yours as ever,

Adina

Dear Lucia,

I am engaged to be married. Yes, I really am. Again. And this time, it's the real thing. I knew I had made a mistake as soon as I realized that my handsome Sergeant Belcore was a baritone. Mummy always told me that, as an operatic soprano, I must wed a tenor, and Nemorino was the only one around, apart from the chorus, and they never have a private life, the poor dears. Yes, Nemorino turned out to be the one. He even enrolled in Belcore's platoon in order to pay for another bottle of Dulcamara's useless plonk. So he had a sexy uniform too. What was more vital, he had a rich uncle who was dead, though I didn't let on to anyone that I knew. The poor lamb didn't know either, so when I bought his enlistment papers back, he thought I was doing it out of love. But I told you he was a bit of a dope, didn't I? It was just as well for him he was a tenor, and rich. Operatic tenors are so often poor.

Sorry to hear your brother is marrying you off to a lord. He may be rich, Lucia, but he isn't a tenor, you say. That can only spell disaster. You must be really mad about it all. I guess you won't be replying to this.

It's been nice knowing you.

Adina.

E. O. PARROTT

Lucia di Lammermoor

Wae, Wae, that I must tae ye tell
　　How Lucy missed her balance;
I dinna ken the Gaelic well,
　　Sae I must speak in Lallans.

Greet, greet, guid folk (that doesna mean
　　Ye send oot love and kisses
But rather that ye pipe your e'en –
　　Och! what a language this is!)

Puir Lucy is a Scottish lass
　　Wha doesna wish to marry;
For Arthur is a lairdly ass –
　　The choice o' brither Harry.

The wicked laird o' Lammermuir
　　Is Henry: he is frichtfu';
He's ta'en fra' Edgar, tae be sure,
　　The lands wha' are his richtfu'.

But Edgar, he is Lucy's jo;
　　In secret they are meetin';

Alas, for Henry comes to know –
    And noo begins the greetin'.

Ae forgit letter someone's writ
    Tae say that Edgar's courtin';
When puir wee Lucy hears of it
    She doesna think it sportin'.

'Come, Arthur!' brither Henry cries,
    'We hae a weddin' plottit.'
Sae fashed is Lucy wi' surprise
    She signs upon the dottit.

But in comes Edgar: 'Sic mistrust,
    Wee Lucy, 's unco petty!'
He joins a sestet o' disgust
    (The opera's Donizetti).

They say a Scottish lassie whae
    Is marryit unwillin'
Will tend tae gang a mite distrait
    And even tak' to killin'.

Her wedding gown is red wi' bluid;
    There's been an awfu' *bad* scene;
Nae panic, lads: the singin's guid:
    This is wee Lucy's Mad Scene.

Nae Doctor Cameron gies aid:
    Wi' wae her heart is riven;
When Edgar hears, he's sair dismay'd
    And joins his lass in Heaven.

It isna Donizetti's plot
    That gars us tae sic pity;
He had it fra Sir Walter Scott
    And changed the names a bittie.

'Lucia' and 'Edgardo' mak
    The tale seem awfu' dotty,
Sae I hae turned the persons back
    Intae the richtfu' Scottie.

PAUL GRIFFIN

Maria Stuarda

It's 1586 and there's a proper little pother
When the Queen, Elisabetta, has Roberto to consider:
Does he love her? Or prefer instead (and this'd be a bother)
Her relative, Maria, a Stuarda – and a widder?

There's some horrid complications, which are nineteen to the
дozen,
For the French King has proposed that he might wed
Elisabetta,
So perhaps it's time – or not time – to decapitate her cousin
(That's Maria, our Stuarda, who is writing Lis a letter).

Now as Leicester (that's Roberto) tells us in a little ditty,
He feels passion and a half for this Maria, the Stuarda;
Without her, his life is miserable. The whole thing is a pity:
He will die if he can't overcome the cruel curs who guard
her.

Her Maj. has two advisers – Talbot's one, the other's Cecil –
And the latter's frankly polishing the Royal Family Chopper,
So we watch Elisabetta as her inward spirits wrestle.
And Maria, our Stuarda, is a prey to those who'd top her.

Out at Fotheringhay Castle, we catch sight of our Maria,
Reminiscing on her youth – *O nube!* – life was so much
sweeter;
Leicester tells Maria: 'Lisabet – be humble when you see her.'
But no matter how she tries it, her emotions soon defeat her.

It's a tongs-and-hammer job, and so the songs are full of
feeling,
As Maria calls Elisabetta 'Anne Bolena's bastard!'
The sopranos leave the audience amazed, agog, and reeling
As the women hurl out insults until both are fairly plastered.

Maria, our Stuarda, has to die. There is a warrant,
Which Roberto tries to stop the Queen from signing. It's a
failure.

She insists instead – and some may think that this is quite
                                        abhorrent –
That he witness execution in his regular regalia.

Now Maria, fully shriven, Leicester feeling close to madness,
Tells her followers they must not weep. The next life will be
                                        better.
Three cannon-shots. They lop her bonce. The audience feels
                                        sadness,
Although history, be frank! – is hardly followed to the letter.

                                        BILL GREENWELL

Roberto Devereux

Elizabeth of England is
In love with Robert Devereux,
Who to her heart returns not his –
You'd think he would be cleverer.

No: Sara's his true Turtledove,
Who Countess is of Nottingham;
And there they go, a-making love
Regardless of who's spotting 'em.

He who rejects his Sovereign's suit,
However good his reason is,
Might guess a ruler absolute
Would say such conduct treason is.

Thus goes, by Queen suspected of
This crime, Roberto Devereux,
To carnifex directed, of
His head to be the sever-er.

                    W. F. N. WATSON

JOHN GAY

The Beggar's Opera

Macheath he was a highwayman
And robbed both rich and poor,
And when it came to ladies he
Was ever so cocksure.

Though pledged to Lucy, Mac got hitched
To Polly, on the sly;
But Polly's poppa rumbled them
And made a plan, whereby

If Mac was hanged, then Polly would
Inherit all his loot;
So he had him nicked, assisted by
Some girls of ill repute.

Now Lucy's dad ran Newgate Gaol,
But Polly's pa and he
Were also into pimping, theft
And such-like villainy.

Young Lucy called on Mac in gaol,
And soon that ne'er-do-well
Had talked her into helping him
To break out from his cell.

His next stop was another ex,
But this gal cooked his goose:
She turned him in – this time Macheath
Was destined for the noose . . .

But no one loves a tragedy
So they let him off the hook;
And Mac reflected, 'mid his molls:
It pays to be a crook.

MORAL

It's odd how some women'll
Fall for a criminal.

RON RUBIN

—— GEORGE GERSHWIN ——

Porgy and Bess

When you've got plenty o' nuttin',
There's nuttin' like drugs, sex and booze
To fill the day
And keep away
Those belly-aching blues.

Although you might try gamblin'
It's likely you will lose,
Or else a knife
Could end your life
If a man won't pay his dues.

Porgy's got plenty o' nuttin',
But shuns such recklessness,
Although he's lame
His honest claim
Is all he wants is Bess.

Bess is a high-flyin' woman,
Though she says she wants him too
Inevitably
And easily
She's led to leave him blue.

Her old lover tries to get her
But Porgy's not standing for that
(Even if he could)

Although he's good
He stabs and throttles the rat.

Porgy's taken to prison
(Though he's killed a murdering crook),
When he's set free
A week after, he
Finds Bess has slung her hook.

Again she's gone with another
To New York's pulsing heart,
But Porgy's brave,
(And to love a slave),
He'll follow in his cart.

Yes, he's got plenty o' nuttin',
And plenty of guts it seems.
Though we have to guess
If he ever gets Bess,
For we're left with just his dreams.

KATIE MALLETT

SIR WILLIAM SCHWENCK GILBERT & SIR ARTHUR SULLIVAN

The Gondoliers

Take a pair of gondoliers
Whom Venetian girls admire
And whose history is strange:
For in childhood, it appears,
One was left with t'other's sire –
The result was interchange.
Take the fact that one's a king
And his friend of humble birth

(Which is which just isn't known)
It's of course the natural thing
 That with all appropriate mirth
  They sail off to share the throne.
Ah! For your true Republican
  It's a most intriguing plan.

Take the daughter to a Duke,
 Of a prince the childhood bride,
  One of those we've spoken of;
Take the amatory fluke
 That the drummer by her side
  Is the object of her love;
Let his so-called mum confess
 That she swapped him in the cot
  For an infant prince – then you
For the general happiness
 Quite a recipe have got
  (There are girls to share it too) . . .
Ah! Since the plot's an also-ran,
  Hear the music if you can . . .

MARY HOLTBY

Iolanthe

When your mother's a fay someone's certain to say, on observing her
 looks and agility:
'Your assertion that this is your Ma we dismiss; such a statement has
 no credibility';
When your filial embrace is pronounced a disgrace by the girl you're
 expecting to marry you,
And she flirts with the peers, and together their jeers are combining to
 mock you and harry you;
You may feel some relief from your fury and grief when the Queen of
 the Fairies enlightens them,
And, a Member 'elected', at last you're respected – nay more, your
 omnipotence frightens them –
You've regained your lost bride, and the fairies decide they will after
 those nobly-born gentry go,

While the Queen of them all is in amorous thrall to the private she's
    spotted on sentry-go . . .
But you haven't won through for though Phyllis loves *you*, the Lord
    Chancellor's scored – he will marry his ward, and is deaf if not
    dumb to the pleas of your mum till she's forced to unveil the
    astonishing tale that the husband she had is this Lord – he's your
    Dad! so he can't marry Phyl but your mother is still as a mere
    mortal's wife under threat to her life till the Queen mends the flaw
    in this Fairyland law and makes weddings that *were* disallowed, *de
    rigueur*, so the peers will explore *terra nova*
And with wings on their backs make immediate tracks for the Chamber
    Above –
And this triumph of love is the sign that the opera's over.

MARY HOLTBY

The Mikado

A wandering minstrel is
        The son of the Mikado;
        He fled, with mad bravado
The bride ordained as his,
And now, in this disguise,
        His native soil he's treading
        The day of Yum-Yum's wedding
(A cause of pained surprise).

Ko-Ko's to be her mate,
        But Nanki-Poo (O sorrow!)
Though death should be his fate
        May have her too (yes, borrow
For four short weeks, until
The Noble Headsman's skill
Be honed to fit the bill
        And cut him through).

But if husbands in Japan have been beheaded
        Then their spouses must be sepulchred alive,
So Yum-Yum, in fact, would rather not be wedded,
        And her lover has no motive to survive . . .

The solution is to pack them off, asserting
    That the execution's duly taken place
(Execution is the punishment for flirting,
    Which accounts for the confusions of the case).

But now the Mikado's come to see
    What's happened to his son,
And when he discovers at last that he
Has supposedly perished by snicker-snee,
    Poor Ko-Ko appears undone.
To lay a siege to a hoary dame
    Don't tickle his dainty taste,
But if he can play the lover's game
And beg the bride who was cast aside,
Then Nanki-Poo is absolved from blame
    And Daddy can be faced.

So no one needs to die
    (Though mentioned in Despatches):
    Matched with appropriate catches
Our heroes bid goodbye.

MARY HOLTBY

Patience

There's a chappy called Bunthorne, all pale and aesthetic,
    Who carries a lily wherever he goes,
With whom twenty maidens (it's truly pathetic)
    Are madly in love, from his head to his toes.
But he loves a milkmaid who's simple and artless
    (To call her half-witted is nearer the mark).
He remains unrequited. It's not that she's heartless,
    But in matters of love she is quite in the dark.
      'Quite in the dark?'
      Quite in the dark.
In love-matters, Patience is quite in the dark.

To complicate matters, the maidens are wooed by a
    Beefy division of Heavy Dragoons,
Who sing, with the girls, in a competent choir
    And march about bellowing Sullivan's tunes.

One of these is a Duke who is worth a king's ransom,
    But is cursed, in his view, with a Thousand a Day.
Enter Archibald Grosvenor, perfectly handsome
    Who draws, like a magnet, the women his way.
        'What is his way?'
        Any old way!
His wondrous attraction draws women his way.

        There is not a lot of plot
        And it's all a load of rot,
        And it's very, very thin,
        So I shall not fill you in.
For in arguments semantic
They dissever the romantic
    With a dis-in-genuous wit.
Their erotic dialectic
Makes their love-lives somewhat hectic,
    Though they never practise it.
        'What never?'
        No. Never.
        'What never?'
        Well, hardly ever.

        For it's all a micky-take,
        Though it makes your sides to ache
When they raffle a Pre-Raphaelitic Poet, who's a fake,
        Though he minces rather pettily
        And Dante G. Rossettily
For he's really just a pushy little bourgeois on the make.

    Each character with passion burns
        (Well, more or less).
    Then, after many twists and turns,
    Dame Hymen's fatal die is cast
    And everyone's hitched up at last,
        They all cry: 'Yes!'
        (Well, more or less).

    So let us sing our Nuptial Chor-
    us, to the figures in this book.
    For Patience gets her Gros-ven-or,

And ugly Jane her loaded Duke.
And everything is for the best,
And all the rest get all the rest,
Except for Bunthorne, poor old Silly,
Who's left communing with a lily –
Except the Wildean Silly-Billy
Who's left communing with a lily.

GERARD BENSON

The Pirates of Penzance

This is the very model of Victorian comic opera,
With girls that flit as lightly as a flight of lepidoptera;
They're the Major-General's daughters, and one of them is Mabel who
Would wed apprentice pirate, Frederic, if she were able to:
He's twenty-one, but still his leap-year birthday makes him under the
Age when from the pirates he can tear himself asunder; he
Wants to be set free from Ruth his former nurse-maid's blunder, but
His word he's given, now the bargain he will never undercut.

These pirates are soft-hearted: Ruth reveals, at last, they're really just
Drop-outs from the peerage who poor orphans always clearly trust;
Now, though crushed by constables who are made to look hilarious,
They're saved from being charged – although their purpose was

nefarious,
But the Major-General cheated them, no orphan he – they're marrying
His daughters, for they're ex-con swells: no plain Tom, Dick or

Harry-ing
Would bring such a remission. Thus the opera lightly ridicules
The powers that be and makes them seem corrupt and snobby, silly

fools.

But still the satire's trapped in tunes delightful to be singing, so
   The Pirates of Penzance will never set alarm bells ringing-o.

MARGARET ROGERS

The Yeomen of the Guard

Our hero Colonel Fairfax has been framed for his inheritance.
A kinsman has accused him and has led the court a merry dance.
And so the Colonel, to frustrate his wicked consanguinity
Decides to take a bride before he's launched into infinity.
A strolling player, Elsie, feels that she is, with her jester, meant
   To be the beneficiary of his last will and testament.
Jack Point, the jester, loves the girl but glumly nods his sicklied head
Provided it's well understood that Fairfax will be quickly dead.

Chorus of G & S-lovers:

Yes, Fairfax will be quickly dead, yes, Fairfax will be quickly dead etc.

The trouble is that Fairfax grows about his Elsie passionate
While mention of his execution Elsie grows quite ashen at,
So when the news that Fairfax's reprieve has been bestowed is sent,
And marriage looks more permanent, then neither of them show
                                dissent.

The happiness which now ensues no shadow overhead impairs
And all the minor characters as well decide to wed in pairs
Except for one who's left alone; while all the others rhapsodize,
Jack Point, by now no longer jesting, feels his heart strings snap, so
                                dies.

Chorus of G & S-lovers:

He feels his heart strings snap, so dies, he feels his heart strings snap,
                            so dies *etc.*

Among the Savoy Operas, this one has no superiors
With Sullivan in solemn mood and Gilbert being serious.
Though not in *Pagliacci*'s class for utter Niobean-ness
It's certainly the closest thing you'll ever find in G & S.

Chorus of G & S-lovers:

The closest thing in G & S, the closest thing in G & S, the closest
  thing in G &, G &, G &, G &, G &, G & S.

NOEL PETTY

PHILIP GLASS

Akhnaten

Philip Glass's Akhnaten
Seems bound to dishearten
As the Pharaoh emotes
On very few notes.

On the other hand
There's plenty of sand,
Though the games that are played
Aren't with bucket and spade,

And worshipping the sun
Isn't totally fun.
(Even in this place
You get sand kicked in your face

And your castles knocked down,
Or, in this case, your town.)
But though Pharaoh's gone,
His spirit lives on.

(As a minimalist
Would like to exist.)

KATIE MALLETT

CRISTOPH VON GLUCK

Orfeo ed Euridice

All is gentle and not screechy
In *Orfeo ed Euridice*:
Orfeo plays the fiddle in
Much the style of Menuhin;

55

Therefore Eros, god of love,
Lets him leave these realms above
And go below to fetch his wife,
Euridice, back to life.
Hellish spirits can't resist
So fine an instrumentalist;
Every barrier to him yields
Right to the Elysian Fields,
Where blessed spirits form a ring
And dance around like anything.

On Orfeo, this great musician,
Eros laid one precondition:
He must never, if he led
Euridice from the dead,
Sneak a look at her, or peek
Even at her lovely cheek.
'Blessed spirits, fond good-byes!
I'll follow Orfeo,' she cries,
But is somewhat disconcerted
To see her husband's gaze averted.
Orfeo tries to keep his calm,
But, panicking at her alarm,
Turns around and, much distressed,
Folds the lady to his breast.
She dies without another sound,
Dropping lifeless to the ground;
Which fills her husband with such woe
He sings a song called '*Che farò*'.
(You surely know it: a heart-breaker
Mostly sung by Janet Baker.
I should have told you from the start
Orfeo is an alto part
Designed for those whose way of life
Is altered by the surgeon's knife.
We do not find such men today.
Is it through NHS delay?
Or reasons I'm content to miss?
Let's finish this parenthesis.)

There's not a dry eye in the stalls

When Orfeo on her body falls
And says: 'The gods combine to spite us!
Yet with this knife I will unite us!'
'Hang on!' cries Eros from the wings;
'Don't say you've had enough of things!
You play the violin so well
It would be wasted down in Hell.
Come, Orfeo, put away that knife,
And, Euridice, come to life.
Get up, you two, and have a dance;
I'll give you both another chance!'

Calzabigi wrote the book
For this marvellous stroke of Gluck.

PAUL GRIFFIN

—— CHARLES FRANÇOIS —— GOUNOD

Faust

Fiends make uncomfortable friends
And sages should be wise to them;
Undue delights have violent ends;
Stained innocence the heavens offends –
Though finally it flies to them.

MARY HOLTBY

Old Doctor Faust within his room
Sits, contemplating suicide,
When, through the all-pervading gloom,
He hears young voices, just outside.

He weeps and dreams of other years –
Of days of women, wine and song;
Then Mephistopheles appears
And slyly asks him what is wrong.

Cried Faust: 'All things I would forfeit,
Provided youth once more were mine,
And I might win Fair Marguerite . . .'
The Devil laid it on the line:

'I can delay mortality
And cast you in a young man's role.
There's just one small formality –
You have to sign away your soul.'

The deal was struck, the deed was done –
Faust is a lusty lad again;
He's off downtown to have some fun.
(The Devil puts away his pen!)

He duly meets Fair Marguerite,
And drives young Siebel from her arms;
And, though at first she's most discreet,
She soon falls victim to his charms.

It does not take him long to put
The lady in the family way,
And then, the chauvinistic brute,
He 'done a runner', as they say.

Some months elapse and Faust comes back.
The lady's brother, Valentin,
Is getting ready to attack –
(He's seen the state his sister's in.)

He swears the family honour must
Be satisfied – and draws his blade . . .
Faust kills him with a single thrust –
(No sweat, with Satan as one's aide!)

Poor Meg – deserted – penniless –
Forthwith she ups and slays the baby!
(Why? Heavens, why? – We can but guess –
Post-natal melancholia, maybe.)

Sentenced to death, she cheats the axe
By dying in her prison cell.
The Devil claims her soul. Relax!
Here comes the Angel Gabriel . . .

*

The tunes are good – 'The Jewel Song',
'The Choral Waltz', 'The Soldier's Chorus',
All help the story line along
And, though familiar, seldom bore us.

Moreover, in this gloomy tale,
Guidelines are proferred which apply
To every discontented male
Weighed down by *anno domini*.

Don't grumble though you're tired and sick –
You have to learn to like or lump it.
Don't make agreements with Old Nick,
Or, in your dotage, dote on crumpet!

T. L. MCCARTHY

—— GEORGE FREDERICK —— HANDEL

Semele

Is Handel's *Semele*
The sort of work to which you can take your Aunt Emily?
Well, there are no scenes of nudity,
But Jupiter does behave with the utmost lewdity.
Personally, I think a god should be permitted to have the morals of a
tarantula
Without being asked to conform to standards that are avuncular, or in
this case auntular.
In fact, Handel didn't write *Semele* for performance
Or to show that gods behaved like Mormons;
(Not that wenchery
Upset the Aunt Emilys of the eighteenth century),
But because at the time all operas
Were floppers;
So Handel, always one for money and glory-o,
Wrote *Semele* as an oratorio,

59

Which enabled his singers to describe acts of the utmost sensuality
Without upsetting the guardians of public morality
By stirring thoughts that would not otherwise have occurred to
   Female relatives of the type hitherto referred to.
The plot is neither complex nor spidery,
Being about Jupiter's bit-on-the-sidery;
If, Semele says to him, I have to submit to the hurly-burly
Of being your favourite girly,
Tell me why I can't see you as you really are. Tell me, if *you* know!
(She has been put up to this by Juno,
Who, as the unwanted lady on the scene,
Is not exactly Mrs Clean.)
So what happens when the mortal looks on the immortal?
Conflagration; and the smoke of a beautiful friendship disappears out
   of the portal.

MORAL

A rival's advice in a matter that's amatory
May well be misleading, or even inflammatory.

PAUL GRIFFIN

ENGELBERT HUMPERDINCK

Hansel and Gretel

Young Hansel was a decent lad,
And sister Gretel wasn't bad;
And yet, before my story's through,
You'll be quite shocked by what they do.
While strolling through a leafy glade,
They came upon a cottage made
Of rather tempting gingerbread.
'Let's eat some, Gretel,' Hansel said.
They didn't pause to think at all
But tucked into the outer wall.
A woman, well advanced in age,
Came rushing out in quite a rage.

'How dare you eat my house?' she cried.
The frightened children tried to hide.
'I'm baking cakes,' she said with glee.
'I'll add you to my recipe.'
She seized both children by the hair
And dragged them in – O luckless pair!
Then to the oven she turned back.
The children launched a swift attack.
The oven door they opened wide
And pushed the angry crone inside;
They slammed the door, turned up the heat
And cooked a crispy teatime treat.

To vandalize a property,
And bake till brown an OAP,
Are surely not, I hear you say,
A normal part of children's play?
Such conduct, violent and rude,
Was caused by lack of proper food.
For Mum and Dad were rather poor,
And when their milk spilt on the floor,
They'd nothing left but empty shelves.
The children had to feed themselves
And gain what nourishment they could
By picking berries in the wood.
Subsist on berries! Please don't try it!
They hardly form a balanced diet.
And no one's adequately fed
Who merely nibbles gingerbread.
Yet that is all poor H. and G.
Consumed for breakfast, lunch and tea.
No vitamins at all that day!
No D! no C! no B! no A!
Research has shown what that leads to:
Aggressive conduct, low IQ.
Small wonder in so short a time
Those innocents should turn to crime.
For children who have had their fill
Will seldom vandalize or kill;
But souls are led into perdition,
When bodies suffer malnutrition.

MORAL

To save your children from such sins,
Just feed them Multivitamins.

KEITH NORMAN

—— LEOŠ JANÁČEK ——

The Cunning Little Vixen

Deep in the woods, waking up from a snooze,
A forester sees a young fox. He pursues
The beautiful vixen, and makes her his pet,
And she grows up to be a vivacious brunette.

One day she escapes, much to his distress;
He tries hard to catch her, but has no success.
She browbeats a badger, takes over his den,
And meets a fine fox: has a family. Then

Along comes a poacher – she fancies she'll steal
His basket to augment the family meal;
But a fox is to him just inedible meat –
No Friend of the Earth, he shoots her *tout de suite*.

In his senescence, the forester spies
A vixen cub just like his lost one; he tries
To capture the creature, but to no avail –
And that is the end of this curious tale.

RON RUBIN

Jenůfa

JENŮFA'S DIARY

July 25: An amusing afternoon at The Mill. Everybody was there.
Grandma Buryja, wearing a calf-length black dress and red kerchief,

was peeling edible tubers, while my cousin Laca, fetchingly attired in a loose lilac blouse which he wore *au campagnard* over dark baggy trousers and boots a size too large, was whittling. Jano, in sheep-skin *gilet*, put his head round, to tell us he could now read. Even the mill man made an appearance, subtly attired in a loosely belted flour sack, very *à la mode*. He sharpened Laca's knife and was kind enough to pay me a compliment.

I was rather missing Steva, whose child I am expecting, but he too turned up, well turned-out in a scarlet tunic with an embroidered strip down the join. He had apparently been whooping it up at Annabel's, and arrived with a party in variegated military uniform, with contrasting cummerbunds, all somewhat the worse for champers. Steva was the life and soul of the party.

Unhappily my stepmother, Kostelnička, wearing an off-the-shoulder blouse and a rather *passé* dirndl skirt with a ruched elastic waist, made an unladylike scene, saying that Steva may not marry me till he's been sober a year. This does not augur well for our expected child's legitimacy!

Later we all had a sing-song. Then everybody cleared off and I was left alone for a heart-to-heart with Steva, who was suffering a bit from the booze, and frankly, I didn't get much out of him. After he'd gone Laca came back and completely ruined my p.m. by slashing my cheek with his knife.

Jan. 5: Mainly taken up with needlework and chat. Baby is well and looks divine in blue babygrow with matching bobble hat. Kostelnička, still in her summer outfit, was on good form and I took a little dope with her and passed out. I have a confused idea that Steva must have called. Pity I was so spaced out, because it's the first time he's called since Baby was born. Also seem to have heard Laca's voice. Very little recollection. What was in that stuff?

Jan. 7??: A bit hazy about the date. So much has happened. People have been in and out. Steva's apparently engaged to Karolka, the mayor's daughter, of all people! Laca seems to have got over stabbing me (lucky him!) and is now affectionate again. I've accepted his proposal (any port in a storm!) And to top it all, Baby is dead. And buried. All this while I was zizzing! Whatever was in that stuff? Terrible weather.

March 14: Wedding Day. Something old (hand-made lace shawl), something new (red sarafan, sewn by Kostelnička), something borrowed

(Granny's locket), something blue (sash). I decided to do without a corsage but Laca brought in a lovely bunch of daffs and I couldn't resist. Steva came in, looking splendid in an apple-green balloon-sleeved shirt, side-fastening at the neck and voluminous black satin pants tucked into rather macho bucket-top boots. He brought his fiancée, looking sweet in a somewhat over-embroidered bodice in conflicting pinks. After they left we all sang a song. Granny was in great form and had put on her Russki doll triangular headscarf specially for the occasion.

Suddenly there was a great hue and cry! They found a drowned baby in the mill stream. Trust the thaw to come today, of all days! Even naked I was able to recognize the child as my own. I was asking for some species of explanation, when the crowd (in generalized pea-sant costume) turned quite hostile. Then, of all things, Kostelnička claims to have murdered him! What a day! Murdered him to help *me*, would you believe? Apparently she thought him too like Steva (though, personally, I couldn't see the resemblance) and thought he'd dog my footsteps! Anyway she'd told Laca it was dead to improve my chances! The nerve of some people!

Well, it's been on-off, on-off, but I suspect I'm stuck with Laca now.

GERARD BENSON

SCOTT JOPLIN

Treemonisha

In Dixieland the slaves were freed
By Lincoln's regiments of blue.
Yet what could hapless black folks do
With alien liberty? Their creed
Was magical and superstitious.
What leader with a steadfast hand
Would guide them to the promised land?
The vital spark was Treemonisha's.

A foundling child from Arkansas
Who set herself, when just sixteen,
The task of an evangeline,
She preached against the voodoo lore;
She mocked the grip of superstition.
True knowledge that would raise her race
To its deserved and equal place
Inspired Treemonisha's mission.

The conjurors who feared her schemed
To seize the girl whose fiery plea
Had jeopardized their wizardry.
Such punishments for her were dreamed
As death upon a hornets' nest.
But, as in any wholesome play,
Her friends arrived to save the day,
And all concluded for the best.

BASIL RANSOME-DAVIES

RUGGIERO LEONCAVALLO

I Pagliacci

Cutting from Circus Times *(incorporating* The Ringmaster*) Milan, 1892*

REVIEW: *I PAGLIACCI*

I am afraid I came to this performance under a misapprehension.
The title – *Clowns* – led me to expect just that, namely some good
old-fashioned baggy-pants humour in the knockabout vein. Un-
fortunately, it turned out to be anything but that; instead, we had
jealousy, tears and murder set in a circus troupe. Moreover, for
some strange reason the whole thing is sung (or at any rate sobbed)
to music which is about as far removed from *The Entry of the
Gladiators* as it could be. The composer is someone called Leon-
cavallo, who apparently does this sort of thing all the time.

The leader of the troupe, Canio, is consumed with jealousy over

Nedda, his wife. Tipped off by Tonio, an equally jealous fellow-clown, he almost surprises her in *flagrante* with Silvio, a villager. In the show that evening, Canio departs from his role and threatens Nedda to make her reveal her lover's name. She refuses, whereupon Canio stabs her with a somewhat carelessly placed knife. Silvio springs to her aid from the audience, but also falls to Canio's knife. The show closes with Canio's words: 'The comedy is over.'

To my way of thinking, the comedy never got started. And Canio didn't look much of a joey to me; he was certainly no quick-change artiste, either, taking up a large part of the first act just getting his make-up on.

Not many laughs, then. No performing seals to make up for it, either. There is a serious point to be made here, though. If the mammas and the pappas get the idea that this sort of thing is going on behind the canvas, what happens to our reputation for family entertainment? Fortunately for our profession, though, I can't see a show like this ever achieving any kind of popularity, so perhaps we should ignore it, as I'm quite sure the public will.

NOEL PETTY

PIETRO MASCAGNI

Cavalleria Rusticana

You need not fear
Mascagni's *Cavalleria*;
The tale's Sicilian, but the music's pleasant.
Santuzza's heart
Is really torn apart
By losing Turiddu, her handsome peasant.
The jealous Lola,
Before Alfio stole her,
To soldier Turiddu her troth had plighted,
But though they married
The marriage has miscarried,
And he and she long to be reunited.

It's Easter Day;
We hear the organ play;
The village celebrates the Resurrection.
They go to church;
Santuzza, in the lurch,
Pleads with her former love for his affection.
Alas! the hound
Just throws her to the ground,
Angrily telling her she mustn't fret so.
Alfio swears
He'll feed him to the bears,
And we are left to hear the Intermezzo.

When church is over
Turiddu asks his lover
To drink with him outside his mother's pub.
'*Viva il vino!*'
He sings; and he and she know
Alfio will regard this as a snub.
Any Sicilian
Will turn a bright vermilion
When anybody monkeys with his wife;
And here's Alfio
Who comes to make a trio
And call Turiddu to defend his life.

They're off to duel.
'On Easter Day! How cruel!'
Cry all the women; most of all his mother,
Waiting in fear
And trembling to hear
Which of the duellists will kill the other.
There's no relief;
The opera ends in grief:
Santuzza's future looks distinctly patchy:
Turiddu's killed;
With screams the stage is filled;
Then there's an interval, then *Pagliacci*.

PAUL GRIFFIN

—— JULES MASSENET ——

Manon

Manon Lescaut is a beauty, young and innocent to boot;
On her journey to a convent, she steps off the coach *en route*.
Cousin Lescaut whom she meets at Amiens has promised to
Furnish her with moral guidance – tell her what she mustn't
do.

Manon Lescaut looks around her at the ladies of the town,
At the tavern's lively patrons – at this waistcoat, at that
gown;
Then she spies a perfect stranger ('perfect' quite describes the
man!)
The *Chevalier Des Grieux* (say in French, to make this scan).

Manon Lescaut and Des Grieux quickly realize that fate
Has arranged this special meeting – so farewell, the convent
gate!
Soon he's whisked her off to Paris, to a cosy lover's den.
(Some pre-marital indulgence was permitted, even then.)

Manon Lescaut is a beauty – we've established that before –
And she proves a great attraction to the nobleman next door,
Who (with Cousin Lescaut's aid – now *he's* turned out a
proper cad!)
Has her lover-boy abducted – so she joins him in his pad.

Manon Lescaut is the undisputed Queen of Paris now
And the gamblers, rakes and libertines queue up to make
their bow.
From the gilded cup of pleasure our proud beauty drinks her
fill –
With her noble patron standing by, to settle up the bill.

Manon Lescaut has been told that Des Grieux is back in
                                                    town,
And about to take his final vows – she gives a little frown.
'What a frightful waste,' she warbles. 'Mimi, fetch my
                                            feathered hat!
My sedan chair at the double! I'll soon put a stop to that!'

Manon Lescaut and Des Grieux are arrested at a rout,
He for cheating at the tables, she for 'putting it about'.
Ladies, then, of easy virtue were transported overseas;
And the magistrates quite frequently ignored 'Not guilty'
                                                    pleas.

Manon Lescaut, under escort, to Le Havre is despatched,
Outward bound for Louisiana. An escape plot has been
                                                hatched:
Des Grieux and Cousin Lescaut (He's turned up again, you
                                                    see!)
And a gang of their supporters plan to set the lady free.

Manon Lescaut hears the shots that put the rescue team to
                                                    flight,
But the sergeant of the escort, sympathetic to her plight,
Lets her have a moment with Des Grieux just outside her
                                                    cell.
She expires in perfect order, with a tuneful last farewell.

                            *

Prudent parents, if a convent for your daughter has been
                                                planned,
Choose a suitable establishment that's fairly close at hand.
Unaccompanied girls in transit pose a risk one can't ignore –
Get the Very Reverend Mother to collect her at your door.

                                        T. L. McCARTHY

— GIAN CARLO MENOTTI —

The Telephone

Cutting from Communications Engineering, *New York, 1947*

REVIEW: *THE TELEPHONE*
by Gian Carlo Menotti

This is a brief one-act opera with a plot which, though slight, has profound implications for the communications industry: it hinges entirely on the use of the telephone. Let us hope that it will be the precursor of many grander works on this noble theme.

In the opera, Ben wishes to propose marriage to Lucy, but she is perpetually occupied on the telephone, and he must shortly leave to catch a train. After trying to sabotage the telephone in his frustration, Ben gives in, proposes by telephone and is accepted.

The telephonic equipment used in the production is a simple conventional black Bakelite handset. However, I was able, by timing the pauses in the recitative while dialling takes place, to deduce that the switching system employed was of the Strowger type, with a genuine cylindrical-arc ten-by-ten array; and that the carrier system was probably set up to derive 18 circuits from two nonloaded 19-gauge cable pairs. There were a few instances in the plot of both wrong numbers and crossed lines; these will no doubt be largely eliminated from future operas as the more reliable cross-bar systems come into wider use.

The experienced communications engineer will probably learn little from this opera that is new, but as a herald of things to come this reviewer found it a most stimulating and exciting evening.

NOEL PETTY

AARE MERIKANTIO

Juha

A Finnish opera, performed at the Edinburgh Festival in 1987.

Marriage to a backwoods peasant,
    Long of tooth and halt of hip,
Seemed to Marja *so* unpleasant
    That she gave the sap the slip:
Came one day a hawker-hiker,
    Dazzled her with shawls and brooches,
So she scarpered with Shemeikka –
    Free from Ma-in-law's reproaches.
Next we see her waiting for him
    In his fishing hut, and there
Come three girls who all adore him,
    Quite content his love to share.
Seems that after every summer
    Yet another lass appears;
Only Marja, latest comer,
    Greets the news with angry tears.
These have plentifully soused her
    Ere we see her with his child;
Seraphina comes to oust her –
    Consequently pretty riled,
Home she goes to patient Juha:
    He will rear Shemeikka's brat;
Goes to fetch it – what a hoo-ha!
    Scoffing Daddy's knocked down flat.
Simple Juha thought his missis
    Kidnapped, not a willing mate;
Otherwise informed, he hisses:
    'Is it true? You couldn't wait
For my death?' She can't expunge
    Truth, nor its effect diminish;
Disillusioned hubby's plunge
    Proves the work's, and Juha's, *finish*.

MARY HOLTBY

— CLAUDIO MONTEVERDI —

La Favola d'Orfeo

When Orpheus, Apollo's son, the poet and musician,
Was told a snake had killed his young wife, Eurydice, he
Pursued her down to Hades and, by guile, obtained admission
And charmed Old Pluto into setting Eurydice free.

One condition! Leaving Hades, if he once looked round,
The deal was that he'd lose his wife – it came as no surprise
When Eurydice (when he'd peeped!) was dragged back
    underground
And broken-hearted Orpheus flew back to Paradise.

In Monteverdi's version all the action is conveyed
By chanting declamations between each and every song;
Imagination only is intended to parade
Earth, Hell and Heav'n before us as the story rolls along.

But this is not quite good enough for latter-day productions;
Where Hades is projected with a laser-beam device,
And flights from Earth to Heaven – well, they have to seek
    instructions,
And ask a man from *Peter Pan* for technical advice.

And one producer recently, of highest reputation,
He really overdid it . . . but we must be careful here!
We understand he's sensitive and fond of litigation –
We certainly have no desire to have *him* round our ear!

We're sure that should we circulate a damaging aspersion,
Solicitors would be employed to harry and to irk us.
Suffice to say, throughout the trade, his very trendy version
Was known to all concerned as Monteverdi's Flying Circus!

T. L. MCCARTHY

L'Incoronazione di Poppea

When Nero, in thrall to Poppea,
Elected to crown her his peer
   Octavia, his spouse,
   With thunderous brows,
Decided she'd best interfere.

She enlisted the wisest around,
Old Seneca, who would expound
   To anyone near
   That Nero's idea
Was not constitutionally sound.

But Nero replied to this play
By ordering *felo de se*.
   Poor Seneca, loyal
   To anything royal,
Obligingly had to obey.

Octavia now made a date
With Otho, Poppea's true mate,
   To find somewhere shady
   And murder that lady,
Restoring Octavia to state.

The immortals now entered this thriller:
The God of Love halted the killer,
   And Poppea smiled
   At Octavia exiled
And Otho fobbed off with Drusilla.

With nobody left to cause strife
Poppea became Nero's wife.
   They lived ever after
   In lecherous laughter
Which doesn't seem fair, but that's life.

NOEL PETTY

— WOLFGANG AMADEUS — MOZART

Così fan tutte

DAMON RUNYON VISITS THE OPERA

Last evening I am passing the opera house minding my own business when I see Big Sammy standing in the doorway looking more than somewhat annoyed. Now, Big Sammy is not such a guy as I wish to have any part of so I look at the sidewalk and hurry by, but as I do so he grabs me by the collar and hauls me in. I say how pleased I am to see him and make to move on but he tells me that his ever-loving wife has failed to meet him and as he does not like watching opera alone he wishes me to use her ticket. Of course, I do not wish to watch this opera and even if I do wish to watch it I do not wish to watch it with Big Sammy, because he is always doing discreditable things such as stealing from people or sticking knives in them, but he insists and naturally I do not wish to give him any argument so we go in.

We are watching something called *Così fan tutte* which Big Sammy tells me means they all do it. I am thinking that this is something about dolls which is known to all and sundry but naturally I do not say so to Big Sammy. Then the orchestra starts up and I wave my hand in time with the music, but Big Sammy says this is something customers do not do, so I stop. Then the curtain rises and two officers named Ferrando and Guglielmo are in a restaurant drinking and comparing their ever-loving dolls. They are singing in a foreign language which I do not understand and to tell the truth do not much care to hear, although I do not say so to Big Sammy, but I am able to follow because it is all explained in the programme that he has bought me. These parties are about to depart for the wars and are claiming that their dolls, who by the way are called Fiordiligi and Dorabella, will in no way cheat on them while they are away. Now, with them is a bookie called Don Alfonso who lays odds that these dolls will take the wind in no time at all, although he does not say what these odds are.

In the next scene Don Alfonso calls to tell the ever-loving dolls that the officers are going away, although I do not see why he does this because they come in to tell the dolls themselves. They warn the dolls not to fool around and of course the dolls are telling them how much they love them and are weeping, although I notice that their make-up is not running.

Next scene there is a maid, Despina, who is in cahoots with the officers, who come in dressed as Albanians and canvass each other's dolls. I think to myself that these dolls must be dumb at that, because first they do not recognize their own guys' faces and voices that they have been seeing and listening to only five minutes before, and then they do not recognize their own maid when she comes in dressed as a doctor. She does this because the Albanians pretend to take poison when the dolls turn them down and she magnetizes them to life, which is something I have not seen done before and indeed do not believe. When they are once more on their feet they start canvassing again, and it appears that the dolls are beginning to weaken.

In the second act the ever-loving dolls come to the conclusion that they will forget Ferrando and Guglielmo and instead will display their shapes to the Albanians, and I must say that they are very nice shapes indeed, if you care for shapes. The maid comes in disguised as a lawyer and once again the dolls do not recognize her, which I find strange indeed because I recognize her at once and I do not even know her. She draws up a marriage contract which is music to the dolls' ears but frightens the lovers who run out of the joint before you can say scat. But they come back dressed as themselves and are by no means pleased at what their ever-loving dolls have been up to. But Don Alfonso tells the tale of what has been going on and the officers forgive the dolls and all ends happily, especially for Don Alfonso who has won his bet, although we are never told what the odds are and how much scratch he collects from Ferrando and Guglielmo.

DEREK ROBERTS

Don Giovanni

Sir W. S. Gilbert, feeling that Leporello's cataloguing abilities are not sufficiently exercised in Mozart's opera, supplies an additional aria, using Sir Arthur Sullivan's well-known music from The Mikado.

As Don Giovanni's servant ('s good a master as I've found)
I had to keep a list – he made me keep a list,

This society philanderer who now is underground,
Of all the girls he's kissed – how many girls he's kissed.
There are lots in France and Italy, and '*mille tre*' in Spain,
Is Donna Anna one of these? The story isn't plain:
The Commendatore (that's her dad) is skewered by the Don;
Elvira's hell-bent on revenge (she plays the jilted one)
And Don Ottavio has got his knickers in a twist;
Old habits still persist – I've got to keep a list.

Then there was gay Zerlina who's to be Masetto's wife;
The Don has got *her* fixed – she *must* go on his list –
Who's overawed, and oversexed, and tired of peasant life;
A party'll get them pissed – she'll join the list when pissed.
But with the party in full swing the vengeful three arrived,
Unmasked, and saved Zerlina from the fate the Don contrived;
The party ends in disarray, the Don escapes with style,
Goes on to woo Elvira's maid (Elvira *I* beguile),
Then Masetto, duped and jealous, suffers boot, and knee, and fist:
The Don's a pugilist – a noted pugilist.

The Commendatore's statue speaks – oh God, he'll come to dine!
I hoped he'd not insist – I hoped he'd not insist;
He hammers on the door between the pheasant and the wine;
This ghost's a moralist – a deadly moralist.
But Don Giovanni won't repent; the women he's seduced
Are worth the sulphurous flames of hell; he'll never be excused.
Elvira begs in vain, and the Commendatore wins.
Dragged down by female harpies to atone for manly sins,
Don Giovanni's now an archetype, loathed by the feminist,
And on their blackest list – at last he's on their list!

D. A. PRINCE

The Magic Flute

Tamino, pursued by a snake,
Gets lost in a wood by mistake;

The Queen of the Night
Recites her sad plight
And begs him to help for her sake.

Her daughter Pamina, she sighs,
(And hints that the girl's quite a prize)
   Is held by a priest
   From the mystical East,
Sarastro; Tamino complies.

She gives him a magical flute
That cures any ill with one toot.
   Papageno, a chap
   Who nets birds in a trap
Goes along, as the comical coot.

On reaching Sarastro's domain,
The high priest turns up to explain
   The two must go through
   An ordeal or two
Before they can pop the champagne.

The first task they must overcome
Is of staying immovably dumb.
   Pamina appears
   To pour balm in his ears,
But Tamino declines to succumb.

Papageno, a less noble man,
Finds a pretty young maid, whom he can
   Summon up or dispel
   By ringing his bell,
A rather convenient plan.

Tamino meanwhile perseveres,
Dismissing all semblance of fears,
   Surmounting all grades
   Of flames and cascades
Familiar to stage engineers.

At last all the suffering done,
The magical lovers are one;

Sarastro is seen
To be wise and serene
And the Queen disappears in the sun.

Some say that it's all hieroglyphic,
And the symbols Freemason-specific.
Since I'm not of that sect,
They may be correct,
But it's fun. And the music's terrific.

NOEL PETTY

The Marriage of Figaro

Cutting from Illustrated Vienna News, *1786*

REVIEW: *THE MARRIAGE OF FIGARO*
BY A LADY

After his *Il Seraglio*, which was escapist in every sense, it is good to see Herr Mozart turning his attention to matters of serious social concern. *The Marriage of Figaro* is a particularly bleak tragedy, dealing with one of the great evils of the present day, the servant problem.

The opera opens on preparations for the wedding of Figaro, Count Almaviva's valet, to Susanna, the Countess's maid and ward. The Count's wedding gift is to be the room in which we now see them. Lavishly furnished as it is and occupying the entire proscenium area of the National Theatre, I cannot help thinking the Count has made a mistake here. If you once give an inch to servants, they will take everything. But there is worse to follow.

The Count, bent on exercising his *droit de seigneur* on Susanna, tries to delay the wedding. Marcellina, the housekeeper, also claims to be engaged to Figaro and a postponement is enforced. Meanwhile Cherubino, a most impertinent page, is amorously inclined to almost everybody. I am sure we have all met this type. He is posted off to the army, most properly in my view.

Ultimately the Countess and Susanna conspire to exchange clothes to expose the Count's foolishness. The final act of confused identities involves the entire *menage* including the insolent Cherubino (who, incredibly, is still here) and various members of the outdoor staff. Figaro having been shown to be

Marcellina's son, the Count, shorn of all authority, caves in and allows the wedding.

The effect of all this sordid *verismo* is even more harrowing than kitchen sink drama, for here we observe not merely low life, but the explosive effects which inevitably follow when above and below stairs are allowed to mix. While I would not condemn *droit de seigneur* on wishy-washy liberalistic grounds, it does entail a degree of familiarity with the lower classes that I believe we should avoid.

At the root of this ghastly mess is the sinister Figaro-person, whom one might best describe as a not-quite-a-gentleman's not-quite-a-gentleman.

There is a lesson for us all here. With more discipline, and rigid application of the iron rule of 'no followers', Count Almaviva's tragedy need not have happened. We are all in Herr Mozart's debt for the unflinching realism of his warning.

NOEL PETTY

Il Seraglio

Mrs Elton Enlightens Emma on the Joys of The Seraglio

'Do you know the music of *Il Seraglio*, Miss Woodhouse?' Mrs Elton asked. 'I am exceedingly partial to it. Mr E. and I visited Bath in the barouche-landau from "Maple Grove" to hear it performed in concert at the Assembly Rooms.'

'The only Mozart I have is for the pianoforte,' said Emma.

'What a pity!' Mrs Elton replied. 'My *caro sposo* might have been persuaded to sing one of the arias of Belmonte. But I will tell you the story – you may imagine the music. It is all about a Turkish pasha who is holding the lady Constanze and her English maid, Blonde, in captivity. He has bought them from pirates who have abducted them from Spain . . .'

'Poor little Miss Smith was nearly abducted by Gipsies . .∴' began Mr Woodhouse, from the card-table. Mrs Elton was not to be diverted by Harriet Smith, a person of no consequence and went on: 'The Pasha means to make Constanze his chief wife, though she resists his advances. At last, Constanze and Blonde are rescued by their fiancés, Belmonte, who has posed as an architect to get into the palace, and his servant, Pedrillo, at dead of night . . .'

'Young ladies,' said Mr Woodhouse, 'should not venture out at dead of night, they could catch a dreadful chill . . .'

Mrs Elton ignored her kind host. 'The lovers escape unhurt,' she said, 'and the droll old steward, Osmin, who had intended that Blonde should be his (laughing affectedly) handmaid, or slave-girl, is thwarted. Pedrillo has drugged his wine . . .'

'A very little wine, taken in a glass of water . . .' began Mr Woodhouse, only to be thwarted in his turn by Mrs Elton who continued: 'When the Pasha, in spite of the fact that Belmonte's father had once wronged him – the "Architect" has revealed his true identity – sees the devotion of Belmonte and Constanze, he allows all four lovers to go free. He is very gentleman-like for a Turk . . .'

Emma looked at Mr Knightly despairingly. She feared Mrs Elton's narrative would never end.

'Shall I ring for supper, Emma?' he said, and added: 'Your sister must acquire the music of *The Seraglio* for you in town. We are sadly behind the times here at Highbury!'

'There is nothing wrong with Highbury, Knightly,' said Mrs Elton, 'that cannot be put right by such as we, doting on music and good conversation as we do!'

MARGARET ROGERS

MODEST PETROVICH MUSSORGSKY

Boris Godunov

(*Who Murdered his Way into the Kremlin, but Ended up Losing his Onions*)

The chief defects of Boris G.
Were Murder, Lust and Treachery.
These minor blemishes apart,
He had a Pure and Noble Heart.
As in-law to the reigning Tsar,
The throne So Near and Yet So Far,

He amplified his claim to power
By chucking off a Kremlin tower
Young Dmitry, the outstanding heir,
Who made his splashdown in Red Square.
Thus, when the Tsar gave up the ghost,
Boris was First Man Past the Post.

Meanwhile, one Grigory, a monk,
Had shed his cowl and done a bunk
To Poland, making himself known
As Dmitry, heir to Russia's throne.
A Local Lass, Princess Marina,
Sniffing a chance to make Tsarina,
Promised him in the moonlight dim
That she'd Espouse his Cause (and him).
The Poles fell in without discussion,
Glad of a chance to Bait the Russian.

Boris, back home, was Up to Here
With spectres, wraiths, remorse and fear,
Hallucinations, superstitions,
Frenzied dreams and apparitions;
Not at all the Sort of Thing
The People look for in a King.

Eventually a Man of God
Recounted something rather odd:
A shepherd who had lost his sight
Had, in a vivid dream one night,
Been told to pray by Dmitry's crypt
And was with vision re-equipped.
Hearing the sound of Dmitry's name
Poor Boris, Overcome with Shame
And generally filled with dread,
Cried out aloud and Fell Down Dead.

MORAL

Little boys who are unkind
Can be driven from their mind.

NOEL PETTY

— JACQUES OFFENBACH —

Orpheus in the Underworld

The violinist Orpheus
Prefers his cat-gut to his wife:
No more hyper-uxurious
Eurydice's a source of strife.

Lascivious Eurydice,
In hot pursuit of *uomo tutto*,
By subterranean odyssey
Fuels luxurious lusts with Pluto.

Public Opinion fulminates
Envisaging malign distortions:
She knows that scandal escalates
To true Olympian proportions.

Jupiter lays priapic plots,
But loss of powers theocratic
Means younger gods debating lots
Of brave decisions democratic.

I see th' Olympian brood descend
In high Bank-holiday jubilation:
As moral voyeurs they attend
Eurydice's new liberation.

Hell's fury's less than woman's, bored:
Boetian Styx bores more than man can.
Like manna come the god-like horde
Who learn at Pluto's feet the can-can.

Dry Orpheus does not deserve
Eurydice, who's hot and hearty:
Fly Jupiter with greater verve
Finds her a most seductive party.

Opera's solutions sometimes miss
Public Opinion's expectations,

And logical hypothesis
Is scotched by later revelations.

Orpheus's backward glancing – so! –
Breaks (to his great relief) the tryst;
Eurydice remains below
In joyous Bacchanalia, pissed.

D. A. PRINCE

The Tales of Hoffman

As a bloke with an eye for the dames
(I love every inch of their frames),
I had quite a ball
With three I recall.
(I can even remember their names!)

A doll named Olympia danced
Till my eyes were completely entranced.
I gave her a whirl,
But alas! the poor girl
Came to grief as our romance advanced.

In Venice I met Giulietta;
I'd have given my soul, just to get her:
On reflection I see
She wasn't for me,
For she loved shiny baubles much better.

Antonia really could sing,
But she also was weak, the poor thing!
One day she felt tired,
The next she expired,
And that was the end of that fling.

My latest is Stella. I fear
She's just like the rest, the poor dear.
Though she's asked for a date
I'm afraid she must wait,
For I'm stuck with my muse, and my beer.

KATIE MALLETT

—— GIACOMO PUCCINI ——

La Bohème

Life in an attic
Attracts the romantic;
Banter and antic
Oust every care . . .
Hand-hold ecstatic,
Exit of gumption,
Mortal consumption –
Everything's there.

MARY HOLTBY

Rodolfo and Marcello
With many another fellow
    Are going on the spree;
Rodolfo is a writer,
A pretty casual blighter
    Who's starving in Paree.

Rodolfo burns his writing
To supplement the lighting
    And help him warm his feet;
The rest in high bonhommy
Go off to drink consommy;
    He'll join them for the meat.

A seamstress from the attic
Is really quite emphatic
    She needs her candle lit;
He sings, once he has seen her,
    'Che gelida manina!'
    ('How cold your tiny mitt!')

'*Si. Mi chiamano Mimi,*'
She tells him. 'Come and see me
  And my embroidery.'
Rodolfo loves her beauty,
And cries: 'It is your duty
  To come and live with me!'

They go and join the jolly;
It's far from melancholy
  Down in the local square.
Marcello sees Musetta
Who thought she'd got a better –
  An aged millionaire.

But now she finds she's weary
Of having to be cheery
  To such a sobersides,
So, flirting with Marcello,
She walks out on the fellow –
  Well, actually she rides.

Two months go by; for Mimi
A life that seemed so dreamy
  Has started to go off;
Both couples tend to bicker,
And Mimi's growing sicker
  With a very nasty cough.

In scratchy saturation
And loving devastation
  All four are in a daze;
And so they think it better
For Mimi and Musetta
  To go their separate ways.

One day Musetta, crying,
Brings little Mimi, dying
  For both the men to see;
The news is hardly merry:
Her trouble's pulmonary;
  In fact, she has TB.

Some search for food and heating,
While, as at their first meeting,
Once more Rodolfo cries:
'*O bella signorina,
Che gelida manina!*'
Poor Mimi laughs, and dies.

PAUL GRIFFIN

The Girl of the Golden West

She was loved by all, where coyotes call, the Girl of the Golden West,
For the miners knew she was pure and true, with a heart of gold in
her breast.
She'd keep *their* gold from the robbers bold, and them from going
wrong,
This backwoods girl, this 'Polka''s pearl, who ran her saloon with a
song.

Minnie had been the 'Polka''s Queen since her Dad, the boss, had died;
And though Sheriff Rance fancied he'd a chance of making her his
bride,
He made her sick – unlike young Dick who showed up at her bar:
They'd met before; Rance was sore that Dick outshone *his* star.

But Rance was told Ramarrez bold, the leader of a band
Of robbers who the miners knew snatched the gold from the grafter's
hand,
Was skulking near. They left their beer and Minnie to give chase;
Minnie was glad and soon she had asked Dick back to her place.

They were deep in love. The heavens above sent a storm, so Dick
must stay
In Minnie's hut the whole night but their joy turned to dismay,
For a hullabaloo meant the miners knew Dick was leader of the pack,
Ramarrez; though she was shocked to know, Minnie hid him in her
shack.

He blamed his Dad and said he had turned over a new leaf:
Not touched the gold that he'd been told she kept for the men; a thief

Henceforward he would never be, for he loved her most sincerely.
She'd not forgive; he'd no heart to live, went out and was shot dead —
nearly.

She was horrified, dragged him inside to hide in her loft above;
The Sheriff, Rance, found him there by chance as the blood dripped
from her love.
To save him yet Minnie made a bet to play Rance a poker game:
Her love at stake, a chance she'd take; she cheated without shame.

Rance yielded his prize, but the miners, wise to Dick's whereabouts,
got their man,
They would lynch him for this was the law of the wild Californian;
But just as the rope was tightened, hope was kindled in Dick's breast,
For to his side rode his future bride, the Girl of the Golden West.

She begged the men for the sake of when she cared for them like a sister
To set Dick free, in the future he would be her honest mister.
They bade goodbye to the pair; each eye, as they watched them go,
was wet,
For never again would these wild west men see the girl they'd not
forget.

You may think a girl like an unflawed pearl is too good to be true in a
place
Where girls were sold for a digger's gold, especially the fair of face;
You may think that Dick's change of heart was quick, if not distinctly
frantic:
But what the hell, most operas tell tales desperately romantic!

MARGARET ROGERS

Madama Butterfly

THE NEW MIKADO

PINKERTON: A wandering sailor I,
Devoted to malarkey;
My wife in Nagasaki
Is Madame Butterfly.

I hired a bungalow,
    Three servants, and a missis;
    A fine arrangement this is,
Until I have to go.

But when away to the sea I steal
    (With her! the American Eagle)
I look for a wife that's a bit more real,
    And my heart is Kate's
    When I reach the States
In a way that's just as legal.
    Hey ho! hey ho!
And hey! the American Eagle.

BUTTERFLY: Taken from my family,
    Married to a naval Yankee,
Told I must a Christian be,
    Done up like the Widow Twankey;
Surely never did you see
    A victim of such hanky-panky;
Fifteen, and a Japanee,
    Married to a man called Frankie!
Sticking up for loyalty
    I keep a knife inside my hanky,
Destined, I may say, for me;
    Murderess I am not, thankee!
Taken from my family, etc.

SHARPLESS: A more humane American Consul
    Was never in Nagasaki;
      I fear the Lootenant
      Is flying his pennant
      In waters somewhat sharky;
It is my very best undertaking
    To ease and simplify
The sad heartbreaking
That Pinkerton's making
    For poor little Butterfly.

I do not want to force
This couple to divorce

But that I fear is the only course,
The only possible course.
Since he's deceived his wife,
I fear she'll use the knife
And one of the two will lose a life,
Will terribly lose a life.

All you who watch the opera story
Of Butterfly's grief and pain
May think that Puccini
Is rather a meanie
To make my efforts in vain.
You have to honour the Japanese lady
For staying true to her man;
She will not divorce him
Or struggle to force him
To follow the laws of Japan.
But Butterfly has a baby boy
Which, when she bows to fate
And, broken and weary,
Commits hara-kiri,
She leaves to Pinkerton's Kate.
The moral, I think, is easy to follow:
It's an old Red Indian law:
An American brave
May not always behave,
So PIN YOUR FAITH TO HIS SQUAW!

I did not want to force
This couple to divorce
But that I fear was the only course,
The only possible course.
Since he's deceived his wife,
I feared she'd use the knife;
And so she did; and she lost her life,
She terribly lost her life.

PAUL GRIFFIN

Manon Lescaut

Readers of Daisy Ashford's *The Young Visiters* will recall that at the end of chapter seven, on the first night of their 'week of Gaierty' in London, Ethel and Bernard set out for a 'little table d'ote followed by a theater', but no account of the evening follows. Recent scholarship has unearthed a missing chapter.

A NIGHT AT THE OPPERA

We will go to Convent Gardens, the famous Oppera House said Bernard as they savioured their coffie. Oh yes said Ethel how romantic. As they dissended from their hansome the Oppera House was ablaise with light from chandleers without number, eluminating the flowers in the famous gardens.

The oppera is Manon Lescoe said Bernard the people are French but the words are Italian because the composer Mr Perchini hales from that country. Do not worry I will explain it to you he added kindly. He looked very hansom in his stiff shirt.

After the overtour the opening seen took place at an inn where Sargant Lescoe was on his way to put his sister Manon in a convent because she was to fervolous. At the inn a rich gentleman called Geronty persuaded Manon to run away with him to stop her from being too bored in the convent but before they could do so a gay young galant called Day Greer came in who was more hansom so Manon illoped with him in stead in Geronty's carriage.

Ethel wispered to Bernard that Manon did not seem at all well brought up, but Bernard said it is the French way my dear they are very lax.

In the next seen Manon was living in sumpshus splender in Geronty's house in Paris. She had sperned Day Greer because he had no money left to buy her jewels and mantels but he still visited her in secret. Then Geronty discovered them and called the police to have Manon arrested as a cortisone. Her brother warned her first but she dallied to gather her preshous jewels and was caught. Bernard said this showed how fervolous she was, but Ethel thought that she would not like to leave costly jewels behind either.

In the intervle Ethel asked Bernard what a cortisone was but he went very red and dashed off to the bar for some more champain.

In the second half Manon was sentenced to be departed but Day Greer persuaded the captain of the ship that was departing her to take him also as one of the common semen. In the last seen Manon and Day Greer were revealed parched and starving in a dessert near New Orlions. When Day Greer went off to find water Manon thought he was gone for ever and he returned to find her dyeing of despair. She expired in his arms declaring her eturnal love for him. Day Greer then expired also.

Ethel cried all through the last seen. Bernard was very embarrassed and lent her his silk hankychief. He apologized for proposing such an unsuitable entertainment but Ethel said no she thought it was very beatiful and perhaps she would like to be a cortisone some day.

So ended Ethel's first night of Gaierty.

NOEL PETTY

Tosca

Trust no fuzz, nor pull the leg
Of one who's ardently attached;
Sweethearts still may be dispatched.
Chickens counted in the egg
Aren't invariably hatched.

MARY HOLTBY

Cutting from La Gazzetta della Polizia, *Rome, 1900*

REVIEW: *TOSCA*

It is no exaggeration to say that Sgr Puccini's latest offering has dealt one of the severest blows to the cause of community policing that has been felt in recent years. As if our task were not already hard enough, he has depicted the police in a light which can only suggest that he bears them some ancient grudge of his own; perhaps a boyhood brush with an over-zealous constable in Lucca?

Be that as it may, the Police Chief in this case, Scarpia, is shown entering a place of sanctuary without a warrant; arresting the 'artist' Cavaradossi on suspicion; supposedly subjecting him to brutal and unauthorized methods of interrogation; extracting information by threat from the prisoner's lover, Tosca; and seeking a bribe of her sexual favours in return for the prisoner's release. In all of this, the girl and her lover, together with their associate the 'political' prisoner Angelotti (presumably a euphemism for urban terrorist), are shown in the most sympathetic of lights, with the police representing the forces of evil.

Now we've all known one or two bent coppers, but this portrayal of Scarpia goes right over the top. Moreover, one bad apple doesn't spoil the whole barrel, but no credit at all is given in the opera to the backbone of every police investigation, the bobby on the beat.

We would earnestly advise Sgr Puccini to make a few changes before the show goes on tour. For instance, the prisoner could be cautioned and questioned by two detectives in full view of the audience, so that there could be no suggestion of undue pressure; and Scarpia's stabbing by Tosca would become a premeditated attempt by her to spring Cavaradossi from prison. At the very least, an Act IV should be added which would show the proceedings in the police inquiry which would inevitably follow the unfortunate misunderstanding over Cavaradossi's firing squad. Such an accurate exposition of police methods as they really are could only enhance the educational value of the opera.

NOEL PETTY

Il Trittico

Cutting from the Brooklyn Bugle, *1918*

REVIEW: *Il TRITTICO*

I fear your critic arrived a little late for the opening of Mr Puccini's new opera, and was so busy trying to grab a seat that I forgot to get a programme. The plot of this piece therefore took quite a bit of working out, but I'm pretty sure I've got it straight now.

Michel, a bargee, finds his wife Georgette is being unfaithful to him with Louis, a longshoreman. Louis mistakes the glow of Michel's pipe for Georgette's signal and boards the barge. Michel strangles him and hides him under the cloak, so that when Georgette comes to shelter under the cloak from the night air, she gets the corpse full in the face. So far, so good.

The next act opens on Sister Angelica in a convent. This seems like a pretty drastic change of gear until you realize that this must be Georgette who's taken the veil out of remorse. Naturally, she has a new name, and you can't see her face for the cowl anyway. We hear she had an illegitimate child (presumably Louis's kid) so I guess that fits the remorse theory. Anyway, Sister Angelica has a visit from a rich aunt who wants her to renounce some inheritance in favour of her sister, who is about to marry. The aunt happens to mention that the kid has died. Sister Angelica is burned up by this news and takes poison. This is apparently a mortal sin, but she offers a prayer to the Virgin and everything turns out OK.

In the final act we change scenes again to the bedroom of a rich *corpus delicti*. The relatives are stunned to find that the old man has left all his property to a monastery. I guess this must be the monastery where Sister Angelica died, and maybe this was the inheritance her aunt was talking about which the old man has since switched. Anyway, one of the relatives, Rinuccio, sends for the local rogue, Gianni Schicchi, who impersonates the dead man to the lawyer and changes the will. The joke is that he changes it in his own favour and the relatives can't do a thing.

I had some problems here, because it was obvious from where I was sitting that Louis and Gianni Schicchi were the same guy, and likewise with Michel and Rinuccio. Then I figured that maybe Louis escaped not quite dead, and maybe Georgette divorced Michel and married Louis before she became Sister Angelica, so Louis was after his ex-wife's share of the old man's loot. Michel, of course, would be on the run for the supposed murder of Louis, so he disguised himself as Gianni Schicchi.

My only serious criticism is that it seemed to me that Mr Puccini never quite decided whether he was writing a tragedy or a comedy. But the tunes are good, and it certainly kept the old brain cells ticking over.

NOEL PETTY

Turandot

THE CASE OF THE CHINESE OPERA

I had been at the opera for well over three hours before Holmes slipped into the seat beside me. Indeed, the singing had stopped, the heavily costumed singers were walking forward into the flares, and applause drowned the footsteps of the escaping orchestra. I was about to speak but Holmes silenced me with a wave of his hand.

'No, Watson,' he hissed, 'you do not need to recount the details. To the trained mind the plot, fiendishly oriental though some may find it, is elementary.

'Take that man, for instance,' he pointed at Calaf. 'He stands confident: he is a hero, successful in love. His strange garb proclaims foreign birth, while the richness of the decoration suggests some position in his own society, perhaps even royal blood. Tartar, perhaps. His eyes have that wakeful, unsleeping quality often found in men of that race.

'That old man is probably his father. He has a defeated air. Parents, Watson, often try to restrain their progeny from impetuous acts – note his right hand, still clutching his robe. The servant girl, perhaps a slave – barbaric societies, Watson, have none of our progressive ideas – has suffered: her crumpled rags indicate rough and violent handling, while those smears of blood around the fifth thoracic vertebra point to severe bleeding leading to death, possibly by her own hand. But at this distance . . .' He frowned in irritation across the darkness of the dress-circle as the applause rattled on.

'By Heaven, Watson,' he exclaimed suddenly, 'I have it! See those three Chinese characters – state servants, I warrant, from their bureaucratic uniform. And finally that woman – now, what do we know of her, Watson? High born, from the whiteness of her skin, and proud: look at her head-dress. Inscrutable, highly strung: the sort who'd kill a man who dared to love her. Unless he could find the solution. An enigma, Watson, a whole set of riddles.' Absorbed in inner speculation he watched Turandot take her bow.

'But,' he said in triumph, his face clearing, 'she has capitulated. Her riddle is solved, as all good cases should be, Watson. She will go with the stranger, the one successful in love.'

I shall never cease to marvel at Holmes' deductive powers. No man

I have ever met could piece together a story from such meagre evidence.

Leaping to his feet, to the consternation of the good woman to his right, he clapped me on the shoulder. 'Come, Watson,' he cried. 'Let Lestrange find us another case before dawn.'

He pushed between the packed bodies, who still applauded with vigour. I followed more slowly, pausing only to pick up the cheaply printed cast-list and synopsis that slipped from the pocket of his greatcoat.

D. A. PRINCE

—— **HENRY PURCELL** ——

Dido and Aeneas

I never thought he was easy, that P. Vergilius Maro;
His hexametrical metre made reading the fellow a nightmare.
It doesn't surprise me that Purcell, with Tate to write the
                                    libretto,
Setting some Vergil to music, decided to do it in English.
Arms and the girl, he sang. The girl was the fly in the ointment.

Dido and Aeneas tells of events when a party of Trojans
Land, like a package of tourists, upon the North African
                                    coastline,
Where Queen Dido rules lands, known to the Romans as
                                    Carthage –
Intasun, Thomsons, Horizon call it Tunisia these days.
She falls head over heels for Aeneas, Prince of the Trojans;
He too is madly in love, and wanting some gratification,
As would you, if you'd left your home and your city in cinders,
Having to carry your old Dad out of the place on your
                                    shoulders,
Travelled around long years: no place you could possibly go to,
Then dropped – plonk! – in the arms of the dishiest queen in
                                    the business.

Should he marry the girl? or take what he wants and be going?
Act One sings about this, and has him deciding on marriage.
'Wonderful news!' sing all ranks; so Aeneas goes out with the
                                                    boarhounds!

Act Two: an echoing cave's the scene for a coven of witches
Plotting to pass Aeneas phoney commands from Olympus.
Regardless of Animal Rights, our hero has cut off a boar's head,
Meaning, no doubt, to retain it, and cook some pork for his
                                                    supper.
Lost in a terrible storm, away from his friends and companions,
Mercury, really a witch, tells him it's time he is going –
   Going, I mean from Carthage, leaving his love in the process:
'Take to the boats and away! drop whatever you're up to!'
Aeneas sadly accepts.
                    It's worked like a charm.
                                        Well, it *is* one.

Aeneas's sailors have wives all over the African coastline;
They don't give a cuss about leaving, and sing a rude chorus to
                                                    say so.
All this starts Act Three. They'll be ready to sail before
                                                    morning.
On come the witches in glee, and dance a gavotte with the
                                                    sailors.
Only poor Dido is sad now, knowing Aeneas is leaving.
Just for one moment he wavers: then he goes off to the
                                                    seashore.
Dido sings us the song by which we remember the opera:
'When I am laid in the earth, remember me, Prince of the
                                                    Trojans.
Remember! remember!' she cries, then dies to the moans of the
                                                    chorus.

Oh, what a terrible tale! written, I'm told, for a girls' school.
How must the poor little things have flooded the gym at the
                                                    ending!
Still, Rome had to be founded; otherwise those little girlies
Would have shed many more tears, having to study Etruscan.

Not that I think he was easy, that P. Vergilius Maro.

PAUL GRIFFIN

── GIOACCHINO ROSSINI ──

The Barber of Seville

Rossini's *The Barber of Seville* starts with the overture to Rossini's *The Barber of Seville*. This is a work no one has ever had any difficulty in recognizing, except Rossini himself, who intended it for something completely different. He is usually said to have taken the story of the opera from a play by Beaumarchais called *The Barber of Seville*; but in fact he took it from an opera called *The Barber of Seville*, which was very well known until Rossini got to it.

The opera opens in the street under the heroine's window, where Count Almaviva is being a devil in Seville. To be precise, he is serenading Rosina, the future Countess Almaviva. She is the ward of Dr Bartolo, a bass by profession who, like the Lord Chancellor in another famous opera, is not in the business of giving agreeable girls away. Rosina is a very agreeable girl, and a mezzo-soprano with a gift for coloratura.

Figaro now enters and announces that he is a Factotum, which, to judge from his patter aria, means that he runs a barber's shop for upper-crust Spaniards. Anyway, he works for Dr Bartolo, and is therefore in a position to help the Count obtain ingress.

By posing as a drunken officer, Almaviva quickly obtains this ingress. In our world he would equally quickly obtain egress, but in Seville drunken officers are apparently quite normal visitors, and it takes a lot of singing before Almaviva is removed. In fact, they have to use a crescendo to get him out. When you hear one of Rossini's crescendos, you will understand the force of this.

Meanwhile Rosina, not knowing her lover is in Debrett, thinks he is called Lindoro. Bartolo, on the other hand, knows he is called Almaviva, but does not know what he looks like. Don Basilio, Rosina's snaky music teacher, advises Bartolo to spread a scandal about the Count, which will gain in volume like . . . well, like a crescendo. This is a very noisy Act.

In the next Act, Almaviva has got his ingress back, disguised as a supply teacher – Don Basilio, by some accounts, having reported sick. The Count gives Rosina a music lesson in Bartolo's presence. With a competent tenor, bass, and mezzo on stage, this is very pleasant, especially when they are reinforced by the baritone Figaro, who arrives to give Bartolo his daily shampoo and shave; but when Don Basilio arrives, not sick at all, it overweights the basses, and everybody sings 'Good evening' to him until he goes off and sings somewhere else.

The lovers plan to elope. However, Bartolo convinces Rosina that her Lindoro is working on commission for Count Almaviva, which makes her so angry that she tosses her Spanish head and agrees to marry her guardian. Bartolo sends for the inevitable notary to perform the ceremony, a storm arrives from the mountains, and Almaviva and Figaro arrive through the window from the street.

All misunderstandings are instantly cleared up, Almaviva and Rosina are married by the notary, and Don Basilio comes back at pistol point to act as a witness.

By the time Bartolo wakes up to what has happened, the knot is tied. He is sufficient of a realist to know that his best course is to look cheerful and hope for a part in Mozart's *The Marriage of Figaro*.

PAUL GRIFFIN

The Italian Girl in Algiers

(*Tune: 'Polly Oliver'*)

O come, you fine ladies and gentlemen so bold,
And hearken to the wonderful tale I'll unfold
Of the fair Isabella, an Eyetalian maid
And Lindoro, her Sweetheart, at sea lost or strayed;
Singing heigh – ho! Windward or lee,
    Where can he be? Lackaday.

This brave Signorina now decided she'd shove
Off over the briny, for to seek her True-Love;
So she hails an old fellow, Taddeo by name
Enlisting his help to seek her old flame,
Singing heigh – ho! Sorrow forswear,
    Farewell despair – *aux quais!*

Sure, the jolly old josser declares: 'Count on me
For to do all I can to be helpful to thee,'
Then o'er the wild waves of the sea their barque steers –

Till it's wrecked in a storm on the coast of Algiers;
Singing Heave – ho! Breakers a-roar
    Wash 'em ashore, Hooray!

Next, they're led off *tout de suite* to the Court of the Bey,
One Mustāpha by name – and there – Oh frabjous day!
What tattoos of delight Isabella's heart gave –
She beholds her lost Love! He's – good Heavens! – a slave!
Singing heigh – ho! Dolour and woe,
    Oh, what a blow! Well-a-day.

But at fair Isabella the Bey takes one peek,
And falls madly in love with her luscious physique;
For she is, he declares, of all houris the Cream,
Just the jewel to complete his belle-bottomed harem,
Singing heigh – ho! bums like full moons
    In gauze pantaloons risqué.

Well, in time they persuade the fond Bey to enrol
As a good '*pappataci*', with only one goal –
To eat and be silent, to be true to the bed
Of neglected Elvira, to whom he is wed,
Singing heigh – ho! No more ox-eyed
    Bits on the side – OK?

And thus Isabella, so resourceful and brave,
Sails away with Lindoro, who's no longer a slave –
Except that forever he'll choose, with no qualms
To be slave to his dear Isabella's plump charms
Singing heigh – ho! Romance and kisses,
    And starry-eyed blisses, Hey! Hey!

W. F. N. WATSON

The Thieving Magpie

Cutting from the Tuscany Twitcher, *1817*

REVIEW: *THE THIEVING MAGPIE*

In *The Thieving Magpie*, Sgr Rossini has once again turned out one of his tuneful trifles. In this opera, Ninetta, a servant girl, is engaged to Giannetto the son of her employer who is the Mayor. When Ninetta repulses the Mayor's lustful advances, he brings her to trial for stealing the domestic silver, and she is condemned to death. At the eleventh hour the real culprit is discovered to be a magpie, and Ninetta is reprieved and married to Giannetto.

Personally I find it hard to accept this version of events. First of all, tableware was said to be involved, which a magpie could only lift with some difficulty. Secondly, if it was a bird at all, a jackdaw would in my view be a more likely candidate; creative artists often fail to distinguish correctly between *Pica pica* and *Corvus monedula*. The former's cry is more of a *chak-ak-ak-ak-ak* than I was able to hear in Sgr Rossini's orchestral interpretation, which resembled more closely the *chack kyaa, chack kyaa* of the latter.

On a more serious note, I do wish human beings could restrain themselves from anthropomorphic condemnation of animals who are merely exhibiting the innate traits of their species. The word 'Thieving' in the title will be offensive to all bird lovers from the professional ornithologist to the weekend watcher.

These caveats apart, and if the opera were to be represented as *La Cornacchia Instintiva* – The Jackdaw Behaving Naturally – there is no reason why the work should not be successful.

NOEL PETTY

William Tell

William Tell is a whizz with an arrow,
But he's miserable, downcast, and glum.
What depresses him through to the marrow?
He is ruled by one Gessler, a bum.
And Gessler, a Habsburg dictator,
Does not mind that the world is amiss,
For he's cruel (which, sooner or later,
Means very hard cheese for the Swiss).

Now Gessler, possessed of a daughter,
Doesn't know up his sleeve there's this ace:
There's a Swiss kid who's trying to court her,
When he should be inspiring his race

To get Gessler. Arnoldo, they call him,
And his princess is lovely Mathilde.
What does Tell think? We see it appal him:
A black look from Tell would have killed her.

But when Melchthal (Arnoldo's old father)
Winds up irrefutably dead,
William Tell whips the lad to a lather,
And he goes after vengeance instead.
Still, Tell, though the Switzers may fête him,
Is strategically really quite thick.
He goes where his foe may frustrate him,
And refuses to bow to a stick.

Now this stick is a symbol of power,
For on top of it's Gessler's great cap,
And though Tell is the man of the hour,
He's arrested, the foolish old chap.
When Tell tells his son: 'Off you toddle,'
Gessler grabs the lad, calling to Will:
'Here's an apple to rest on his noddle,
Shoot it off if you've got so much skill!'

Tell trembles; his son has more bottle.
'There's no need to shake and to shiver!
You're brilliant! Your very first shot'll
Split it clear!' William Tell takes his quiver –
And, bullseye! Core-blimey! Now surly,
Old Gessler calls: 'Both of you die!'
And it's then, 'midst the hurly and burly,
That Mathilde arrives and asks *why*,

Why should Jemmy, the boy, be so treated?
Gessler's stumped for an answer, relents.
But of Tell, Gessler won't be so cheated,
And will feed him to serpents. It's tense.
Now Arnoldo (remember the fellow? –
He was featured way back in the plot)
Gets his chance to disprove that he's yellow,
Which he does, since his ardour is hot.

Where's Gessler? He's taken Tell boating,
To a castle you get to by lake.
There's a storm rises while Gessler's gloating
(You *knew* that he'd make a mistake!)
William Tell leaps on rocks – he's so agile! –
And when Gessler and co. get ashore,
Gessler finds that existence is fragile.
Thus the Swiss rule their cantons once more.

Arnoldo, Mathilde, some peasants
Have little to do in this show:
They warble, and give the thing presence,
But nothing much more. There you go.
Rossini today would have pronto
Been anxious (and puzzled) to ask
Why his audience talked about Tonto,
And his comrade, a man in a mask . . .

BILL GREENWELL

— CAMILLE SAINT-SAËNS —

Samson and Delilah

Once upon a time there was this tribe called the Hebrews who were always getting a lot of stick from another tribe called the Philistines, whom they disliked, because apart from everything else, the Philistines were (yuck) uncircumcised. Then along came a hefty Hebrew hunk called Samson, who was a kind of biblical Rambo, and girding up his whacking great loins, he laid into the blighters and sorted them all out, chapter and verse.

Now apart from his unfashionably long hair, Samson had very little on top, and for a Hebrew his tastes were remarkably Philistine, especially when it came to Delilah, a Philistine *femme fatale* whose sexy routine (known locally as the Gaza Strip) would send him absolutely wild. The crafty old high priest of Dagon – the Philistine god – knew all about these shenanigans, and urged Delilah to use her charms to try and discover the source of loverboy's great strength, which as every schoolboy knows (or used to know) lay in the aforesaid lengthy locks of hair. Delilah didn't need much persuasion, having for some obscure feminine reason gone right off her boyfriend. She lured simple Samson into her love nest, whereupon in rushed a bunch of Philistines. Without so much as a by your leave they gave the poor sod a short-back-and-sides and a nasty eyeball job, then slung him into an insalubrious Gaza jail, where his captors would while away the long hot afternoons by kicking sand in his face, as the mood took them.

One day the Philistines were holding a holy shindig in the Temple of Dagon, and they thought what a good idea it would be if Samson were to provide the entertainment. They dragged him over, and stuck him in the middle of the hall where the high priest and Delilah and the rest of them proceeded to give him a really hard time of it. Samson had had just about enough: he beseeched and besought his God (a.k.a. Jehovah) to give him back his strength, just this once please. Now Samson's God was higher up the divine hierarchy than Dagon (hence the upper case G), and He decided to show Dagon & Co. once and for all just Who was boss. He reactivated, therefore, the Samsonian sinews – and then some. Sam's big moment had arrived: taking a deep breath, he grabbed hold of a couple of pillars which happened to be handy, and CRRRUNCH! – brought the house down.

Well, he'd always wanted to be in show business.

RON RUBIN

THE WORSHIPFUL GUILD OF HAIRDRESSERS, BARBERS, AND TRICHOLOGISTS (ROUEN CHAPTER)
wishes to announce that there is no truth whatsoever in the recent spate of rumours generated by M. Saint-Saens' new opera, *Samson and Delilah*, that depilatory action can cause muscular atrophy or any other diminution of the normal more bodily functions.

HAIRDRESSING CANNOT DAMAGE YOUR HEALTH

NOEL PETTY

ARNOLD VON SCHOENBERG

Von Heute Auf Morgen

At the first night of *Von Heute Auf Morgen*, Frankfurters were treated to a timely political parable on the prevailing state of the Reich.

The couple who, on their return from a party, strike up a domestic quarrel, graphically mirror those divisions among the German bourgeoisie which have prevented their agreeing on a way forward. In the midst of their policy disputes arrives a gasman, wanting payment. This figure is easily identified as a volatile leader of the extreme right (himself gassed in the war) who, having urged his street-warriors into action against the working class, is now presenting his 'bill' to his respectable clients.

Alas, the money has been squandered on fripperies so typical of the bourgeois appetite for vanity and display. But the gasman, though disappointed, will not wait for ever. He will want to buy more serious and practical items than fancy clothes. Already there is a telephone call from a mysterious singer, evidently enamoured of the wife. Who can he be? Those of the audience who stayed awake last night will not fail to associate him with the leader of a transalpine nation (famous for its singers!) who already seeks to woo Germany to his ways.

This person has made a curious bet. Does the light he has seen proceed from the lady's eyes, or from an electric bulb? We might say: from Germany's tradition of art and philosophy or from her resurgent power, which the Versailles treaty cannot arrest? It is over this point that the couple once again argue.

Finally they make up, but this much is clear: their happiness will not last while a dictator and a would-be dictator await their rendezvous. It would be clearer still had Herr Schoenberg chosen a more familiar musical form.

BASIL RANSOME-DAVIES

DMITRI DMITREVICH SHOSTAKOVICH

Katerina Ismailova

(*Lady Macbeth of the Mtsensk District*)

THE BALLAD OF LADY MACBETH

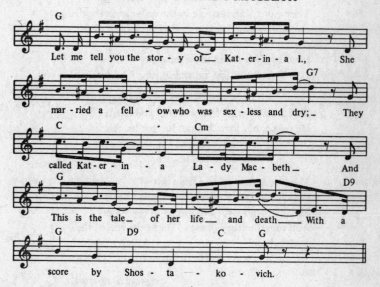

Let me tell you the story of Katerina I.,
She married a fellow who was sexless and dry;
They called Katerina 'Lady Macbeth'
And this is the tale of her life and death
    With a score by Shostakovich.

When her husband's work took him far away,
She made the acquaintance of the handsome Sergei;
First she wrestled with him and then they made love,
But her father-in-law, Boris Ismailov,
    Was suspicious, said Shostakovich.

He not only suspects her, he fancies her, too!
He sings a little song about what he'd like to do;
He catches them at it, gets Sergei beaten,
Then dines with Katerina. What's this he's eaten?
     Why, Poison! says Shostakovich.

So with Pa-in-law mysteriously dead
We find the lovers once again in bed.
The husband returns, starts thrashing his wife;
The pair of them gang up on him and take his life,
     To a tune by Shostakovich.

They conceal the corpse in the cellar with the drink
But a prowling drunkard, alarmed by the stink,
Alerts the police – and their wedding day
Ends by their being trundled away
     To a march by Shostakovich.

Convicts on a bridge. Katerina bribes a guard
To be with Sergei but he's cold and hard.
He rejects her love, blames her for his fall:
'It's your damned fault that I'm here at all!'
     In a song by Shostakovich.

Then he makes up to a little tart
Which cracks Katerina's overloaded heart.
She seizes her rival and jumps in the water
And together they drown. That's the end of the
  slaughter,
     In this work by Shostakovich.

GERARD BENSON

BEDŘICH SMETANA

The Bartered Bride

I mean, this is just another typical example of the exploitation of women in a male-dominated media. I mean, just look at it! There's Mařenka, stupid little thing, succumbing to this man, Jeník, mainly because of his good looks. I mean, what low consciousness! There are so many other life-styles she could have tried: an all-women's collective with shared breast-feeding and crèche facilities &c. But no! She has to throw herself at Jeník. And then there's her *father(!)* trying to plan a rich marriage for her. (OK, the mother too, but only because of the phallocentric society they live in.) Then there's the Marriage Broker (another male) – planning to more or less literally *sell* the girl as a bride for the son of a rich neighbour. I mean, I ask you!

Then it's all arranged! Only trouble is Mařenka won't agree and good for her! But look at her motives: rejecting formal purchase (where at least she'd have a contract and rights) for informal slavery.

Then, to emphasize the theme of subjugation, the whole village dances the polka – with men leading (of course) and the women, of course, giving a degrading leg-show to the stalls!

Act II begins with a Chorus to Beer sung by the men(!) – (so there's going to be a battered bride tonight, as well as bartered). Then there's a discussion (not properly chaired or conducted) between the Broker and Jeník, where they debate the differing ethics of market values and erotic obsession – with little to choose between them. After that we meet the only sympathetic male character (Vašek, a mentally handicapped youth who, it turns out, is the 'husband' chosen by the Broker for Mařenka). She reveals the extent to which she has been corrupted by ridiculing him.

Next, in the most cringe-making scene yet, the Broker and Jeník bargain – literally with bags of money (symbolizing the metallic sterility of the male womb, the money bag), for Mařenka. I mean, Jeník literally gives her up for a financial consideration. OK, so he has a trick up his sleeve but it is so disGUSting. And there's a revolting celebration at the sordid signing of the Contract of Renunciation. I mean, it's done publicly. It's *so* humiliating. The villagers quite rightly take against Jeník, but for the wrong reasons! They believe true love should triumph. I mean. What crap!

Act III points up the whole puke-making theme with the arrival of a circus and another sex-object, Esmeralda the dancer. And by a trick in the plot Vašek's gentle nature is ridiculed by getting him into the macho costume of a bear (that most brutal and man-like beast, *vide* my paper 'Goldilocks, a victim of rape'). In this episode we see naked phallicism (not literally of course) at its most blatant. The link with capitalism is again crudely demonstrated. Mařenka seems to have some consciousness-awakening about her position. She shows commendable anger when she learns that Jeník has apparently turned her down for money. But instead of seeking a Marxist-Feminist solution to her plight, she goes into a depressed state and sings a song about the Spring not being affected by socio-economic factors – apparently unaware of a host of ecological variants brought about by appropriately named 'husbandry'. Then Jeník arrives and really winds her up, telling her to sign the Marriage Contract – and never letting on that he's got the whole thing stitched up in typical entrepreneurial style. Even at this stage she could strike a blow for International Sisterhood. But no, she only signs on the dotted line, doesn't she? Then of course, Jeník is recognized as the long-lost eldest son of the rich man, and wins(!) the bride AND, of course, quite a lot of money. And apparently Mařenka is quite happy with this. I mean, it's one man outwitting another with the woman as chattel. Now for a better way of organizing Bohemian village society we have only to look at the study . . .

GERARD BENSON

——— JOHANN STRAUSS ———

Die Fledermaus

If I had been the younger Johann Strauss,
Would I have called this work *Die Fledermaus*?
This name – *The Bat* – appropriately groovy
For Grand Guignol, or Hammer Horror Movie,
Hardly suggests a schmaltzy sort of jolly
Without a trace of guilt or melancholy.

The central action is a sort of ball,
To which the Prince Orlofsky welcomes all.
The naughty Rosalinda wants to go,
So does her naughty maid, Adéle, and so
Does Rosalinda's husband, who's in stir –

Or that is how the matter seems to her.
In fact Alfredo, Rosalinda's flame,
Goes off to prison in her husband's name.
The Prison Governor, to crown it all,
Turns up disguised at Prince Orlofsky's ball.

And what a ball! So many in disguise
Are singing, dancing, fluttering their eyes;
An aria from Adéle brings down the house,
And Rosalinda's wooed by her own spouse.
Bemused with waltzing and with fizzy wine,
They all sing 'Brother Mine and Sister Mine'.

Last act is in the prison, a gloomy spot,
But not for long, as all pursue the plot.
Though each with wine is variously awash,
No one's as sozzled as the jailor, Frosch.
The Prison Governor's foxed, because he houses
Two men who say they're Rosalinda's spouses.
What does it matter? In Vienna, life
Does not concern itself with man and wife.
This is a prison, not a hermitage;
Adéle, the maid, will go upon the stage,
And till next time, it's living and let-living,
Laughing and dancing, singing and forgiving.

I have not told you why it's called *The Bat*.
It's not too easy to remember that.
A character called Falke's at the ball,
Nicknamed The Bat; he's engineered it all.
From Strauss – Vienna – 1874 –
That's all the logic you can bargain for.

PAUL GRIFFIN

—— RICHARD STRAUSS ——

Arabella

CASE HISTORY: A. W.

The case of Miss A. W. presents various classical features in a highly dramatic form.

On her first visit to my consulting room I found her to be suffering from extreme but disguised anxiety symptoms. She lives with parents who are accustomed to a rich life-style but who are currently struggling, in her own words, 'to make ends meet'. This obviously ambiguous phrase reveals that A. fears her father to be unable to achieve union with her mother. Her penis-envy, combined with her wish to supplant him, is expressed in her claim to have a sister (Z) who is nevertheless perceived as a male, who wears male clothes and who convinces all about her that she is in fact male. This transparent *alter ego* is, significantly, the keeper (preserver) of the door (vagina).

A. claimed to have three suitors of aristocratic birth between whom she could not make up her mind. Also there was a fourth, Matteo, whom in her own person she denied, but in that of her 'male' *alter ego* she sought congress with. It can be seen from the name Matteo (mater/mother) that we are confronted here with a demonstration of the desire to re-enact the primal scene between the parents: the male/female (Z) and the female/male (Matteo/mater). An additional suitor Mandryka (mandrake, the phallic root) both in the person of her father's youthful companion(!) and an illusory figure glimpsed from the window (a young and attractive male) completed the case of this hysterical phantasy.

On her second visit A. described to me a scene at the 'Fiakerball' (the play upon words here is almost too obvious to need explication: a 'ball' for 'balling' i.e. sexual congress). The mysterious Mandryka approached her and made advances, which she did not refuse. She did, however, formally seek time to say farewell to her childhood, most significantly. A further incarnation, the 'Fiakermilli', a doll-like figure sang and danced on her behalf.

However, in her Z. incarnation she was able to give rein to her passion for Matteo, making with him an assignation, in which their dark desire was secretly consummated. This must remain unknown by Mandryka who nevertheless discovered some of these events without understanding them (the riddle).

On her third visit A. described to me the resolution of these events in an aftermath in which Matteo claimed intimacy with her, which she denied (denial syndrome). Mandryka then quarrelled with Matteo (ordeal by conflict of the *animus*) until the Z. manifestation reappeared having voluntarily yielded her masculine disguise (beginning of integration of *anima*). Z. then became a fit and acceptable partner for Matteo (continuation of same). This still left the parental and the A. problems unresolved. However, A. then besought from Mandryka a glass of clear water. In the therapeutic context this, of course, signifies amniotic fluid and symbolizes both her desire to re-experience her birth and also herself to give birth. She then accepted the male principle (integration of *animus*) by offering the 'water' to Mandryka. By this symbolic action both her personal integration and her parents' future were secured.

No further visits were necessary.

GERARD BENSON

Ariadne auf Naxos

All would agree this ancient story lacks os-
  Tensible humour. Theseus was a cad, ne-
Glecting his girl, abandoning on Naxos
    Brave Ariadne.

Now her despair and lamentations rack us,
  How we deplore the loneliness that faced her
Till, to replace the death she cried for, Bacchus
    Softly embraced her . . .

Now to *our* scene: a maelstrom of musicians
  Madly preparing for an *opera seria*
Find that their patron's altered the conditions –
    'Let's make it cheerier!'

Comic relief insultingly is planned, which
      Puts on a par the master and the menial,
Forming, it seems, a kind of *buffa* sandwich,
          Hardly congenial

To the Chief Tenor or the Prima Donna,
      Or the Composer, frantic with frustration:
What will unlettered clowns impose upon a
          Tragic creation?

This: Ariadne wakes from restless slumber,
      Sings of her sorrows – death would be far better;
Then, with her troupe, to dance a lively number,
          Here's Zerbinetta,

Ready to soothe her in her sad abasement:
      'Men are the *end* – the one way to recover
Is to secure immediate replacement:
          Find a new lover!'

Deaf to this sermon – illustrated amply
      By the fair preacher's dissolute behaviour –
Poor Ariadne's still invoking damply
          Death as her saviour;

Greets him, indeed, her love, her crowning mercy,
      When, as she thinks, he comes at last to greet her;
Bacchus it is, who, just escaped from Circe,
          Seems pleased to meet her.

This lovely vision (so he sings) has triggered
      Off in his heavy heart the healing leaven –
While to *her* eyes the island is transfigured:
          Can this be Heaven?

Love is her prize, as love was her undoing –
      Not, Zerbinetta, thanks to your assistance,
Yet you judged right: 'New gods who come a-wooing
          Find no resistance.'

MARY HOLTBY

Elektra

E-lek-tra lives in Greece. She is a Greek girl. She is a prin-cess.

E-lek-tra is not hap-py. She wears dir-ty clothes. Her Dad-dy has gone a-way, and she has a new Dad-dy, called Ae-gis-thus.

Ae-gis-thus does not like E-lek-tra. He beats her. He is cru-el. E-ven her Mum-my, Cly-tem-nes-tra, is cru-el. She wants to shut E-lek-tra in a dark room. Poor E-lek-tra! What can she do?

Lis-ten to the mus-ic. E-lek-tra is sing-ing a-bout her Dad-dy. Not her new Dad-dy, but her old one, A-ga-mem-non. A-ga-mem-non was the King. He fought in the War. Then, af-ter he came home, he went a-way a-gain quite sud-den-ly. Ev-er-y-one was sur-prised. Cly-tem-nes-tra was not sur-prised. Now she is ver-y fat, and has bad nights. This is called in-som-ni-a.

'What shall I do for my in-som-ni-a?' she is ask-ing. E-lek-tra is tell-ing her she must make a sac-ri-fice.

In Greece, long a-go, when you were un-hap-py you made a sac-ri-fice. This meant that you put an an-i-mal to sleep. E-lek-tra thinks it will make her hap-py to put her Mum-my to sleep. Re-mem-ber, she is a Greek girl.

E-lek-tra has a bro-ther, O-res-tes. O-res-tes is a kind bro-ther. He has run a-way from home. Ev-er-y-bod-y says he will ne-ver come back.

'If O-res-tes does not come back, I will make Mum-my a sac-ri-fice,' says E-lek-tra. 'Look, I have an axe.' But no one will help her, not e-ven her lit-tle sis-ter, Chry-so-the-mis.

Now there is a man ask-ing to see Cly-tem-nes-tra. Who is he? Per-haps he is O-res-tes. The man tells E-lek-tra her bro-ther will nev-er come back. He is jo-king. He *is* O—res-tes! He does not know his sis-ter, be-cause of her dir-ty clothes.

E-ver-y-one is ver-y ex-cited. 'Now,' they tell O-res-tes, 'you can make Cly-tem-nes-tra a sac-ri-fice! 'Ev-e-ry-one is hap-py that Cly-tem-nes-tra will be a sac-ri-fice.

Now it is time for your bed. You will not go to bed un-til you see the end-ing? The end-ing is ve-ry Greek. Al-most ev-er-y-bod-y goes to sleep. No-bod-y has in-som-ni-a an-y more. They are all sac-ri-fic-es: Cly-tem-nes-tra, Ae-gis-thus, O-res-tes. And E-lek-tra? She is ver-y hap-py, and goes, ver-y sud-den-ly, to live with her Dad-dy. Her first Dad-dy.

You do not want to be a sac-ri-fice? No. Of course not. No-bod-y needs to be a sac-ri-fice in the Wel-fare State. You have your Soc-ial Wor-ker, Child-Line, and an in-te-gra-ted time-ta-ble.

Please do not make such a com-mo-tion!

PAUL GRIFFIN

Der Rosenkavalier

A discarded consulting room note by Sigmund Freud dated 1910.

Richard S. came to me this morning in a state of considerable excitement. I persuaded him to sit down and tell me of the dream he was babbling about. He responded enthusiastically with the following:

> The young Count Octavian is having an affair with the Marschallin when they are interrupted by a visit from Baron Ochs, her cousin. Octavian disguises himself as a maid. Ochs is seeking an emissary to take the silver rose, symbol of love, to his intended bride, Sophie. Ochs, however, has an eye for the supposed maid. The Marschallin sends Octavian on Ochs' mission, and he and Sophie fall in love. To frustrate Och's intentions, a trap is devised whereby the maid (Octavian) keeps an assignation with Ochs to compromise him in front of Sophie's father. The plan works and the Marschallin graciously concedes her love to Sophie.

This seemed to be wonderful material for my method of interpretation. I explained to Herr S. that the suppressed emotions of his early childhood had been organized by his unconscious self into the figure of Octavian, and the course of the dream suggested that as a baby he had been evidently nursing simultaneous sexual passions for his mother (the Marschallin), his father (Ochs) and his sister (Sophie). The repeated change of clothing by Octavian was consistent with a failure to identify his sexual nature, while the blood relationship of the Marschallin and Ochs was the child's unconscious attempt to place a taboo on sexual relations between his parents. I tried to explore the subject of any incestuous relations between his father and his sister, and was about to explain to him the meaning of the silver rose, when Herr S. grew very impatient and said this was all very well but was I going to

stage it? After some further talk at cross-purposes, it turned out that
he thought I was the theatrical impresario on the next floor. The
whole thing is some kind of opera he has written called *Der Rosenkavalier*, which he is now trying to get someone to produce. I told him
in no uncertain terms that as a stage work it had no chance of success,
since it was in my opinion even more ludicrous than *The Magic Flute*.

And no consulting fee! Things are quite difficult enough without
the attentions of time-wasters such as Herr S.

NOEL PETTY

Salome

> Sex may send you off your head,
> Amorous pleasure may await
> Lightly offered on a plate
> Or through veils which drop, revealing . . .
> May I recommend, with feeling,
> Evenings by the box instead?

MARY HOLTBY

> *Salome*, though distinctly curvy,
> Is not an opera for the nervy;
>   Nor should you show it to a child,
>   For it is based on Oscar Wilde.
>   All characters depicted must
>   Be hopelessly consumed by lust,
>   Except the Baptist, who loves God;
>   Herod desires Salome's bod,
>   So does the Captain of the Guard;
>   Salome wants the Baptist, hard;
>   But fiercely as they all have burned,
>   In no case is the lust returned.
>   Right from the start, one justly fears.
>   The thing is bound to end in tears.
>   This chance is very soon increased;
>   Salome, at King Herod's feast,
>   Performs a wriggly dance so well
>   The King exclaims: 'Oh, what the hell?

I'll give you anything you wish!'
'John Baptist's head upon a dish!'
Quickly replies the vengeful girl.
'Why not a diamond, or a pearl?'
Herod suggests: 'I don't desire
To kill a prophet I admire.'
She makes him do what he has dreaded,
And John the Baptist is beheaded.
When the poor fellow's fate is sealed,
His head is brought in on a shield;
Salome stands and swings her hips
And kisses him upon the lips.
Herod with loathing now is filled.
And quickly has Salome killed.
You will not easily believe a
Company can find a diva
Who, looking like a teenage tart,
Can sing a long soprano part
And act it also – which entails
Dancing the Dance of Seven Veils;
And you are right; they tend to do
This opera when the moon is blue.

PAUL GRIFFIN

IGOR STRAVINSKY

The Rake's Progress

When playing Happy Families
You'll rarely find a pack like these,
For when a life of ease is planned
The devil deals a rotten hand.

Mr Trulove, as his name
Implies, is virtuous; the same
Applies to Ann, his daughter, who
Forever to her love is true.

Tom Rakewell is Ann Trulove's beau,
Who'd rather play than work, and so
He's happy when Nick Shadow comes
To improve his leisure optimums.

Tom and Dick go up to town
(Though morally the path is down).
Respects to Mother Goose are paid –
It isn't long before Tom's laid.

Tom's not content, and Nick, still shady,
Suggests to him a bearded lady
Could make him happy, so the berk
Soon weds the dame – Baba the Turk.

But Baba brings no joy – she prattles
About her various goods and chattels
Till Tom can't stand the noisy nagger,
And with his wig decides to gag her.

Now Sellem, who's an auctioneer,
Comes in to sell off all her gear.
Baba sits quite still, and so
It seems she too will have to go.

She's almost under Sellem's hammer,
When he decides to end the clamour
Of the crowd, and takes her gag.
At once her tongue begins to wag.

It seems a boon for Tom when she
Decides that show biz calls, and he
Is duly grateful for the chance
To find, with Ann, renewed romance.

But at the graveyard Nick discloses
His true identity, and shows his
Winning card – he wants Tom's soul.
It seems Tom's in a hellish hole.

But Nick says he'll negotiate –
A game of cards to seal Tom's fate.
Tom wins, but Nick contrives to send
His hapless victim round the bend.

In Bedlam Tom must sit and rave.
Ann comes to see him – she's so brave.
At last she gets him into bed –
He sleeps, he wakes, he drops down dead.

The moral's finally rubbed in –
To want a life of ease is sin –
You can't outbid the devil's call –
The Protestant Work Ethic's all.

KATIE MALLETT

PYOTR ILITSCH TCHAIKOVSKY

Eugene Onegin

ASK AUNT NATASHA

BOYARS OWN PAPER
MOSCOW

Dear Aunt Natasha,

Six years ago I fell madly in love with my sister's fiancée's best friend, a boy called Eugene. He was terribly handsome and sophisticated and I was just a simple girl. Foolishly, I wrote to him a passionate declaration of love, but he brushed it aside as girlish nonsense. I was so humiliated I thought I would die.

Later on, he flirted with my sister Olga at a dance, and her fiancé Lensky was so jealous that he challenged Eugene to a duel. Lensky was killed and poor Eugene had to go abroad. I have since become happily married to a very nice Prince called Gremin.

Now Eugene has come back. I met him at a dance last week, and he has since sent me a letter saying he now realizes that he is hopelessly in love with me, and will I leave Gremin for him? The thing is, I still love him ever so much. What shall I do?

Worried Tatyana

Aunt Natasha writes:
I have to say that I think you have been a very silly girl. You never

win respect from a man by flinging yourself at his head in the way you did with Eugene. But you do seem to be more sensible now and I'm sure you'll do the right thing.

I'm afraid your Eugene sounds rather a rackety sort of person, and not to be trusted. Are you sure he won't be in trouble for killing his best friend? You wouldn't want to be a prison bride, I'm sure.

Your Prince sounds much steadier to me and I feel confident that if you deal firmly with Eugene now you'll forget about him in time. And it can't be so bad being a Princess, can it?

NOEL PETTY

The Queen of Spades

Herman is an officer, though not it seems a gent;
He's mad on cards and gambling, but never has a cent.
He idolizes lovely highborn Liza from afar,
And then one day he learns that Liza's aged grandmama,
A Countess, knows a way to win at cards, that cannot miss –
(That's why they've dubbed her 'Queen of Spades') – now Herman's
                                                    avarice
Emboldens him, he chats up Liz, and sweeps her off her feet;
She lends the cad her latchkey – an act most indiscreet,
For Herman calls on Granny, waves a gun about her head,
But before he learns her secret, the Countess drops down dead.
Poor Liza is beside herself, and shows her beau the gate,
But later tries to patch things up – alas, the gal's too late –
For Grandma's ghost has just appeared to Herman and revealed
Her famous Three-Card Trick – this is his chance to get well-heeled!
'To cards!' he cries, 'Let's hit the deck!' but Liz is now quite sure
That Herman is a murderer, and flees from her *amour*.
Disconsolate, she drowns herself, whilst Herman cannot wait
To try his luck and see his sinking funds appreciate.
He stakes a stack of roubles on the Three, and as foretold,
It wins – Gadzooks! he'll see his cash increase a thousandfold!
The Seven's next – he wins again! – there's just the Ace to come . . .

But no – the Queen of Spades comes up – now Herman's deeply
  glum;
And when the Countess reappears to taunt and tantalize
The wretched chap, he goes bananas, stabs himself, and dies.

MORAL

Don't be taken in by ghosts: should one appear to you, it
Could be catastrophic – be certain you see through it.

RON RUBIN

—— SIR MICHAEL TIPPETT ——

King Priam

With blaring brass and clashed percussion,
And bars when there's a telling hush on,
Tippett tells the ancient story
Of Greeks and Trojans, in their glory.

It's lust, adultery and war
That fill the stage, with loads of jaw
From women covering the action
As all the men seek satisfaction.

At the end of the day, when all is said
And done, Priam and sons are dead,
The women left to face their plight,
A cheerless way to say 'goodnight'.

If modern music leaves you cold,
No matter what the story told,
Or you can't accept this cup of woe's art,
Just Tippett out, and stick to Mozart.

KATIE MALLETT

RALPH VAUGHAN WILLIAMS

Hugh the Drover

Cutting from The Ring, *London, 1924*

REVIEW: *HUGH THE DROVER*

Mr Vaughan Williams' new opera holds more of interest to the average fight-lover than most operatic offerings. It is set in a small town during the time of the Napoleonic wars. Mary, the constable's daughter, is to be married to John the Butcher, but falls in love with a passing stranger, Hugh the Drover. A boxing match between the two men is arranged, the prize to be Mary's hand. Hugh wins, despite John's attempts to cheat. John then denounces Hugh as a spy, and the latter is placed in the town stocks. Soldiers arrive to take him away, but the sergeant recognizes Hugh as a former comrade, and takes John away to be a soldier instead. Mary and Hugh take to the life of the open road.

The principal interest, of course, centres on the boxing match. The two boys opened warily, the drover throwing a few straight lefts that never pierced the local boy's guard. A short right jab to the ribs had the massive meatman in trouble though, and he responded with a number of low blows and a trip. These had the knuckled nomad staggering, and the ref. should have intervened at this point. The out-of-towner recovered well, though, and eventually the Cotswold carver fell to the flailing fists of the courageous cattleman.

The whole fight lasted 4min 27sec on my stopwatch. Now I know one has to compromise on the stage, but in Jem Mace's time fights used to last for hours, and even now a heavyweight contest can run over an hour if it goes the distance. Surely Mr Vaughan Williams could have extended the fight into the second act, when all that we had to watch instead was Hugh and Mary messing about in the stocks.

I fear boxing is going to remain a poor relation to this generation of operatic composers. Wagner might have done it justice had he lived, but not this namby-pamby lot.

NOEL PETTY

GIUSEPPE VERDI

Aida

There's a little stony pile hard by Memphis-on-the-Nile,
And a little pile of hollow bones within,
So patience, gentle reader, while I tell you of Aida.
Are you comfortably perched? Then I'll begin.

Our hero, Radames, could attain high Cs with ease,
And at every martial enterprise excel.
He was worshipped both by peers and by carriers of spears
And the Pharaoh's daughter smiled on him as well.

But he knew he'd find no bliss with the Princess Amneris:
Aida only made his heart take wing.
But at court she was reviled as a slave-girl, and the child
Of the Pharaoh's foe, the Ethiopian King.

The Ethiopian horde now attacked with fire and sword
And Radames was picked as Egypt's leader,
Which caused the poor chap's brain to reel beneath the strain
Of loving both his country and Aida.

But he quickly acquiesced, and was soon with victory blessed:
No enemy could stand against his skill.
So our hero was repaid with a victory parade
To glad the heart of Cecil B. de Mille.

The Pharaoh's next reward was a somewhat two-edged sword:
As son-in-law brave Radames he'd choose.
Which turned his guts to water – such a gift from such a quarter
Was an offer that you couldn't well refuse.

Amonasro, Ethiop's leader, the father of Aida,
By now a prisoner, thought it well worth trying
To use the love-lorn pleas of besotted Radames
To do a little military spying.

Aida would not bend to deceive her loving friend,
So Radames was with temptation plied:
He was given to understand he could have Aida's hand
As a transfer fee to join the other side.

It was all to no avail; nothing could the pair assail.
But Amneris now entered, black with hate.
And seeing Radames tête-à-tête with such as these,
Denounced him as a traitor to the state.

In the storm to which this led, both the Ethiopians fled
And Radames, though innocent, was doomed.
The council met next day and the High Priest had his way,
With Radames condemned to be entombed.

The solemn music swells, and he says his last farewells;
The stones are ready on the massive set.
But who is this we see? Holy Isis! Can it be?
It's Aida, come to share a last duet.

There's a little stony pile hard by Memphis-on-the-Nile,
And a little pile of hollow bones inside,
And travellers have averred that two voices can be heard
And the interval is just an octave wide.

NOEL PETTY

Ambitious warriors who wallow
In slavish passion are at fault:
Desist, or dire effects may follow –
Asphyxiation in a vault.

MARY HOLTBY

Un Ballo in Maschera

(*After Longfellow*)

In a semi-documentary
Truth becomes a web of lying,
Lies and truth become a hotchpotch,
Lies seem truth, and hotches potches;
So the story of this opera,

Dealing with the King of Sweden,
Couldn't be performed, because of
High Official Repercussions.
In the end, Giuseppe Verdi
Changed the names of all the persons,
Moved the *mise en scène* from Sweden
Right across the Western Ocean
Into Boston, Massachusetts;
Made the Governor, one Richard,
Suffer King Gustavus' murder;
No one cared if *he* was murdered,
For the man was only British.

What was set in Stockholm, Sweden,
Land of lakes and land of mountains,
Needs two gorgeous sopranos,
One to play the pageboy Oscar,
Who's a sort of youthful *compère,*
And the other one, Amelia,
Is adulterously worshipped
By Gustavus, King of Sweden.
She is married to his Secy.,
Anckarstroem, a decent fellow.

In Act I, the King has notice
From this very decent fellow
That some nobles plan to kill him –
Horn and Ribbing are the leaders:
Verdi calls them Sam and Thomas
In the Massachusetts version!

There's a lady who tells fortunes
Out towards the edge of Stockholm;
This is felt to be illegal,
So the King decides to see her,
Check if she could be deported.
As a fisherman he dresses,
Goes to see her, finds she's helping
Poor Amelia find a magic
Herb to exorcise her love for
Him, Gustavus, King of Sweden.

When she's gone, he asks the lady
If she'll prophesy his future.
Less than willingly she tells him
He is likely to be murdered
By the man who next in order
Shakes his hand. Perhaps you've guessed it:
Anckarstroem, the decent Secy.,
Proves to be the lucky fellow.

In Act II, we find Amelia
Rootling round the local gallows
For the magic herb to cure her.
Here the King, her lover, finds her
In the darkness, swathed in veils:
Finds her, woos her, till her husband
Comes and warns him of his danger.
Those conspirators are coming,
Bloody murder their intention.
Anckarstroem is made to promise
He'll escort the veiled lady
Back to safety without making
Any indiscreet inquiry,
And he'll wear the royal mantle,
Leaving his to King Gustavus.
All seems well, till Horn and Ribbing
With the operatic chorus
Enter and insist on seeing
Who the lady with the veils
Really is; they laugh their heads off
When they find that Anckarstroem is
Merely taking home his missus.
Anckarstroem, in furious anger,
Joins the plot against Gustavus.

In Act III the vital question
Is for Anckarstroem to settle:
Shall he kill his wife and monarch?
Shall he kill his monarch only?
First he tends towards the former,
Then he settles on the latter,
Giving scope for lots of singing.

Now the King has turned repentant
And decided to promote him
To a post in distant Finland,
Very properly renouncing
Any claim to his Amelia.
At the Masked Ball of the title,
Waltzing for the last time with her,
He is murdered by her husband.
What a dying scene now follows!
What repentance! what forgiveness!
Not the sort of scene, I fancy,
Often met in Massachusetts,
Met across the Western Ocean,
Where, permit me to remind you,
Verdi had to move the opera!

PAUL GRIFFIN

Don Carlos

LINES TO A DON
(*After Hilaire Belloc*)

Princely but rebellious Don
Whom father, Philip, frowned upon:
Don radical, who's one of those
Who want to aid the Huguenots;
Don didactic, with interests wide,
Don who loved his father's bride
(A Valois girl he's got to know
Whilst hunting up at Fontainebleau).
At first they thought they were betrothed –
A proposition neither loathed! –
(A promise which the King ignores
So he can end his Flemish wars):
Don furious, Don in a rage
(This news is brought him by a page).
Sadly, Elizabeth agrees,
For Valois girls all aim to please.

Don love-lorn, in monastic gloom,
Don beside grandfather's tomb;
Is Charles alive, or is he dead?
No one is certain, so 'tis said.
There stands a monk in shadows dim –
A look-alike? Or is it him?
Don now thinks it's time he chose a
Father-confessor – one Di Posa.
They swear on oath to one another
That each of them will love the other–
Di Posa is one more of those
Who aim to aid the Huguenots.

Don ecstatic (though unwed);
He'd rule in Flanders now instead.
Don now goes to see the Queen,
Although she is his 'might-have-been'.
Will Philip to her wiles but yield
And give to Don his Flanders field?
The King arrives, to join his Queen,
Finds her alone, and makes a scene.
Di Posa comes, a good friend he,
Who chats up Philip cautiously.
The King, he learns, suspects his bride,
And fears Don's suit is not denied.
He cannot trust a man who's chose
To try and aid the Huguenots.

Don now appears through midnight mist –
Don's out to keep a secret tryst.
Don swears he loves Elizabeth –
Don's words could bring Don certain death.
The shrouded figure lifts her veil –
It's Eboli, and Don turns pale.
(She, former plaything of the King,
Is fancying a Donnish fling.)
'You're false!' she raves, and Don now fears
All this may reach King Philip's ears.
The Queen and Posa both appear:
Things get complex and far from clear.

Threats of exposure now go flying,
But no one knows to whom who's lying.
All concentrate upon their woes.
And quite forget the Huguenots.

The scene is now a Seville square,
And everyone who counts is there.
Now Don his resolution shows –
He meets some sample Huguenots.
Inquisitors, it seems, require
That they must perish in the fire.
Don is pleading: 'Not the stake!
They're Huguenots, give them a break.'
Don's apoplectic, Don's arrested,
Don of Don's sword is now divested.
(Di Posa's there to take the blade
Whilst promising his secret aid);
He shows a lot of common sense
By hiding all Don's evidence,
Which brings about the scene's swift close,
And that of those poor Huguenots.

King Philip now bemoans his fate.
What shall he do? His anger's great.
Donate Don to the Inquisition?
Or will the Don express contrition?
The Inquisitor says: 'No' on cue,
And adds he wants Di Posa too.
The Queen gives Philip further shocks –
Don's portrait's in her jewel-box.
His wrath erupts, and then the Queen's
On Eboli, who spilled the beans;
Penitent, that Princess goes
To try to rouse some Huguenots.

Don's lying in his prison cell.
Don's future's bleak, Don's far from well.
Di Posa comes and brings report
Of dreadful news – they are distraught.
Don's secret letters have been found;
Effects of this will be profound.

Don fears the worst. Don's friend is shot
(Before he dies he sings a lot).
The King arrives, and Don is free,
But 'tis no thanks to Eboli.
(It was a local mob who rose;
She could locate no Huguenots.)

The monastery – we hear its bell,
As Don now bids the Queen farewell.
But Philip's waiting in the wings
(A trait of operatic kings),
Don is guilty, Don must die.
(That mystery monk is passing by)
Grandfather's tomb stands open wide,
And so the monk whisks Don inside.
Is Don dead? Well, goodness knows!
Maybe he's joined the Huguenots.

E. O. PARROTT

Falstaff

Dear Marje

I am a shy middle-aged bachelor and I have fallen for two delightful women living near my army billet. As they are both married I am at a loss as to how to make the necessary overtures to them. I feel that it is safer to woo them both as one might be foolish enough to reject me. I should mention that both are married to local tradesmen, but we are living in modern times, after all.

I enclose a recent picture.

John Falstaff, Bart.

Dear Sir John,
I am sure no tradesman's wife would refuse the favours of a titled gentleman like yourself.

Of course I have read of your distinguished war record. I enclose herewith a draft letter which I am sure will suit your requirements.

Having had a second look at your picture, I also enclose a diet sheet and a leaflet on the dangers of over-indulgence in alcohol.

Good luck,

Marje

Dear Marje,
My friend and I have both received the selfsame letter from this rather seedy ex-army man living near Slough. It's not even a very nice letter. All them flowery phrases. Suggestive too. I enclose a copy.
But what should we do?

Yours,
Worried Alice

P.S. My husband wants my daughter Nannetta to marry a dreary doctor who is always getting into scraps with local army louts, whereas she really fancies a nice young man called Fenton.

Dear Alice,
So far as your daughter is concerned, she should follow her heart. I am sure that you can get round your husband one way or another.

As to your own problem, naturally you must feel free to reject any unwelcome addresses, but maybe the fact that other men regard you in this light may strengthen your husband's regard for you. A little jealousy can work wonders with your sex life.

I am also enclosing a little book, 'How to appreciate the art of good letter-writing'. (There is a copy for your friend too.)

Yours,
Marje

Dear Marje,
I think my wife may be going to have an affair with some army fellow who lives in a pub near here. I have it on oath from the johnnie's batman. I thought I might go along to see him in disguise and say I am in love with my wife (which I am not, of course) and ask the chap to put in a word on my behalf. Then I'd get to know his plan and could catch him at it.

Could you please phone me to say if my scheme would work. I am always out between two and three.

Yours angrily,
'A Fontana'

Dear 'Mr Fontana',
I never telephone answers, but I would guess that your regular absences are a temptation to your wife.

Your plan is excellent. I enclose a leaflet about a theatrical costumier.

They have a special department which provides disguises for tax inspectors, bailiffs, spies, men selling dirty postcards or state secrets, etc.

> Good luck,
>
> Marje

Dear Marje,

I took your advice and sent off your letter, but unhappily her husband came back unexpectedly, even though her housekeeper said he wouldn't.

They hid me in a disgusting basket full of dirty clothes, and the next thing I knew I was swimming in the Thames.

Now she wants me to meet her at midnight, and dressed as Herne the Hunter. Does this mean she's kinky? If so, I'm not going.

Sorry about the writing, but I have a filthy cold.

> *Yours bitterly,*
>
> *John Falstaff, Bart.*

Dear Sir John,

Of course you must go. You have clearly aroused her desire. The romantic setting and the costume confirm this. Those horns are, of course, a symbol of sexual prowess and should suit you.

I enclose the address of a theatrical costumier (in which I happen to have shares) and a recipe to cure colds. This was given to me by my grandmother.

> Good luck,
>
> Marje

Dear Marje

The midnight tryst was a disaster and I still have my cold. You and your grandmother both are wash-outs. The woman brought all her friends and relatives along, all dressed as fairies and such. I suppose you and your costumiers made a bomb.

There was even the woman's husband there. He'd been to see me earlier in disguise asking me to arrange some sex for him with his wife. I knew it was a kinky family.

Anyway, the laugh was on him as he betrothed his daughter to the chap she wanted and not the bad-tempered doctor he was so keen on (thanks to my batman).

> *Yours angrily,*
>
> *John Falstaff, Bart.*

(Fragment of letter to Sir John Falstaff. The remainder is missing)

... I enclose details of the Marje Proops Marriage Bureau and Dating
Service. All ladies are guaranteed unmarried ...

E. O. PARROTT

La Forza del Destino

La Forza del Destino is about a long vendetta
    Which is started by Alvaro when he carries off a bride;
Leonora is the lady; she's by no means a coquetter,
    But is very much in love with him, and will not be denied.

Her father is against the match, and catches them eloping;
    By accident he's killed, and he emits a dying curse;
So Leonora's brother, Carlo, swears he'll go on hoping
    To follow Don Alvaro up, and dance around his hearse.

From now until the end of it, they tend to be disguised;
    Leonora puts on trousers to evade her questing brother,
Then Carlo joins the army, and we're not at all surprised
    That now Alvaro's with him, and that neither knows the other.

Meanwhile, the desperate lady has sought and got a permit
    From a good Franciscan Prior whom she tells about her plight
To go into a lonely cave and call herself a hermit,
    With the help of his Community, who pray for her all night.

With the singing of the Brothers, and the singing at an inn
    Where a Gypsy, Preziosilla, sings a patriotic song,
And the singings in the army when the battlings begin,
    And the praying, we are never short of music very long.

There's a good monk – Melitone – who preaches punning sermons,
    And the Gypsy joins the army as a gay *vivandière*;
While Carlo and Alvaro against the Austro-Germans
    Do miracles of valour – an inseparable pair.

But awkward truth in opera has a way of coming out,
    And Carlo and Alvaro now discover their identity;

132

They fight, until their fellows put an ending to the bout,
    And Alvaro runs for cover to a life as a nonentity.

To put his course more clearly, he embraces rule monastical
    In the very same establishment (I dare say you've been guessing)
Where Leonora's daily saying prayers ecclesiastical
    Not half a mile from where her dear Alvaro is professing.

Now on the scene comes Carlo and insists upon more duelling:
    Reluctantly, Alvaro wounds him mortally, and cries
To the hermitage for help; of course, the consequence is gruelling,
    For out comes Leonora to her brother as he dies.

With all his strength remaining, Carlo stabs his wretched sister!
    Alvaro curses destiny (which gives the work its title);
But the dying Leonora, and the Prior to assist her,
    Reassure him, and us also, with a heavenly recital.

PAUL GRIFFIN

Macbeth

In Scotland are a-walking
    Banquo and Macbeth;
They meet some blasted witches
    Upon the blasted heath.

The witches sing in chorus
    And in a spooky tone
A spooky little prophecy
    About the Scottish throne.

The King is going to visit
    The castle of Macbeth;
His hostess sees the way it goes
    And plots the monarch's death.

O mucky is the murder,
    And bloody is the spot!
Macbeth can scarcely say his prayers,
    Which bothers him a lot.

O grisly are the goings-on,
    And Lady M.'s a scold!
But Macbeth's King; and that's the thing
    The ancient hags foretold.

They also said that Banquo
    Would sire a line of kings;
So Macbeth adds his murder
    To all the other things.

They've barely laid the table
    To celebrate his feat
When Banquo's ghost upsets his host
    By sitting down to eat.

They've barely had their starters
    And sung a little toast
When everyone runs off in fear
    To see a hungry ghost.

The witches now are stirring
    A cauldron in a cave;
Here comes Macbeth to ask of them
    How he must now behave.

They tell him to beware Macduff;
    That done, he's safe to reign
Till Birnam Wood shall up and move
    Itself to Dunsinane.

No one who is of woman born
    Can hurt the wretched man.
Does he not know Macduff's Mama
    Had a Caesarean?

O mucky are the murders
    Macbeth commits on all!
And many the Mujahiddin
    That plot the tyrant's fall.

Macduff and Malcolm, raising
    The standard of the sane,
Advance on Macbeth's castle,
    Royal Dunsinane.

They cut the woods of Birnam
    To camouflage their way
And, singing lovely choruses,
    Embark upon the fray.

O terrible the tyrant's rage,
    And hard his Lady's lot!
She walks about in sleep, and cries:
    'O damn this bloody spot!'

The Lady dies, Macbeth is killed –
    He's not been sharp enough,
For one who's not of woman born
    Is obviously Macduff.

What weapon does Macduff employ
    In this? I cannot say more,
For Verdi wrote the death off stage;
    Perhaps it was a claymore.

The opera, ending with a hymn
    Sung by a whole battalion,
Is just what Shakespeare would have liked,
    Had he been an Italian.

For Shakespeare's Scots upon their hands
    Bear only blood and quality;
But Verdi's Scots have little spots
    Of something just like jollity.

PAUL GRIFFIN

Otello

Officers should not depend
Too much on an 'honest' friend;
Envy turns, with evil power,
Love to hatred in an hour;
Ladies die for loss of linen
On the beds they didn't sin in.

MARY HOLTBY

135

Rigoletto

Ribald jesters have to pay,
In the end, for those they mocked;
Girls securely stashed away
Often find themselves unlocked;
Libertines may flourish, whom
Evil men were hired to hack . . .
Taking stock, I would assume
Those intent on deepest gloom
Opt for daughters in the sack.

MARY HOLTBY

A Cautionary Tale on the Inadvisability of Employing a Hired Assassin

Now Rigoletto (we will call him R.)
Was Jester to the Duke of Mantua.
The Duke, you might say, was not half a One
Who liked to have his little bit of Fun.
So of his daughter R. took greatest care
And told her not to go out anywhere
Except, of course, to church. But it was there
The Duke first saw the girl – his 'Unknown Fair'–
And vowed to make her his at any cost.
They met. She fell for him. And all was lost.

She's not the only one who's been seduced,
And Rigoletto's easily induced
To help some courtiers in a Vengeful Plan.
He little knows it is none other than
His daughter Gilda who's to be abducted
And (how ironic!) does as he's instructed.
He has been told it is another lady
Whose goings on have been distinctly shady;
The yarn that's spun is easily believed –
Too late! The Jester finds he's been deceived!

But this is Opera, where Punchinello
Is anything except the Merry Fellow,
And Rigoletto, though it's rather rash,
Hires Sparafucile, who will kill for cash,
To undertake a little spot of murder.
The plot's absurd — and now it gets absurder.

Gilda (soprano) overhears the plot,
But does she get her own back? She does not.
(We should have said before, to make things plainer,
The Duke's abandoned G. for Maddalena.)
The noble Gilda, still infatuate,
Decides to save her faithless profligate
And sacrifice herself. Therefore, in drag,
She's duly shot, and popped inside a bag.

R., all unwotting, takes the bag along,
Then hears the Duke (a tenor) in full song!
The Duke, thinks R., is he who should be dead,
And opens the bag to see who's there instead —
It is his Gilda! From her snow white throat
She summons up her last and highest note,
Before becoming dead and sinking back
Into the dark recesses of the sack.
This cruel twist of cursed Fate appals,
And Rigoletto — and the Curtain — falls.

MORAL

Dear Reader, don't employ a hired assassin
Next time you wish to do a lad or lass in,
Make sure it is the right one who's to die,
Don't pass the buck — just simply DIY.

JOYCE JOHNSON

La Traviata

As a real high-class harlot,
    With sins gilt and scarlet,
They called me *La Dame aux camelias*;
I love a camelia; for one bloom I'd feel ya,
    For a spray or bouquet
    I'd be yours the whole day,
Baron Douphol would say I'm a marvellous, fabulous lay.

    But a life of frivolity
    As tart to the Quality,
Once Alfredo Germont came, went sour;
As our love hour by hour quickly grew to full flower,
    He quite went to my head,
    We were perfect in bed,
To the country we fled, but his Pa made me leave him instead.

    Once again *Grande Cocotte*,
    But soon life's mad gavotte
Must end and can have no resumption;
And that's no assumption, I'm racked with consumption,
    So though gay and high-strung
    When my friends I'm among,
My tubercular lung means my swansong's about to be sung.

    Thus with many a sigh
    On my deathbed I lie,
Weak and wan with this sad hacking cough,
Deep in misery's trough, mortal coil shuffling off –
    But a tap at the door! –
    'Tis my Alf, back once more!!
I can die now life's o'er, in the arms of the man I adore.

W. F. N. WATSON

Il Trovatore

PRELUDE

A baby lived in days of old, reared by a female Gipsy bold,
    Whose name was Azucena.
The Gipsy's child was not her son; her son had been another one,
    Considerably plainer;
And Azucena, in a fit of craziness had roasted it,
    Thinking it was the other:
A serious mistake to make, but caused by seeing at the stake
    None other than her mother.
The foster-baby was the son of Count di Luna – that's the one
    Who burned the foster-granny.
Manrico was the baby's name; he thought the schizoid Gipsy dame
    His mummy, not his nanny.
The Count, of course, like everyone, believed that he had lost his son,
    And shortly raised another.
This boy grew up; the old Count died; the new Count naturally denied
    That he might have a brother.
I have a shock for you, my friend, now that you think I'm going to end
    This complicated story:
I HAVE NOT RAISED THE CURTAIN YET UPON THE TASK I HAVE BEEN
                               SET:

    That's Verdi's *Trovatore*.

ACT I

For the story of the opera I'd better change the metre round:
We start off in a guardroom with the tramp of many feet around
And hear the very story I've been patiently reciting you;
Then to a Spanish garden, which ought to be delighting you.
A casual inquisitor who hung about or hovered o'er
Would find Manrico had become a troubadour or *trovador*.
He has a powerful passion, of a sort you sometimes get in you
To serenade a lady of the Count di Luna's retinue.
In Leonora's garden he will happily disport himself;
Alas! she is a lady that di Luna wants to court himself.

Di Luna comes; he does not know the darkness has his brother in;
The curtain falls before we know which one has done the other in.

ACT II

Bang! bang! the didicoys are striking at the anvil
(Romantic Gipsies as described by Joseph Glanville).
Azucena tells Manrico she is not his ma-ma,
Running through the roasting scene with not a little dra-ma.
Meanwhile, Leonora thinks her lover has been deaded,
And towards a convent with some local nuns is headed.
In fact her fans, despite the rumour, both are well and thriving;
Each with his supporters at the same time is arriving.
Bang! bang! the hooligans each other's heads are striking;
Bang! bang! Manrico finds the outcome to his liking.

ACT III

A hell of a war has broken out, it cannot be denied,
Though Leonora, to her delight, is going to be a bride;
But in the castle where she's been taken, Manrico is surrounded,
And the days of their likely honeymoon appear distinctly bounded.
The Count arrests old Azucena, condemns her to the stake.
Now which of two decisions is Manrico going to make?
To stay in the castle with Leonora, or rescue his foster-mother?
No doubt the former would be our choice; but of course he takes
the other.

ACT IV

Miserere, miserere, Manrico's fate is pretty hairy,
    His and Azucena's:
Captured by the Count di Luna, they have lost their *buon fortuna*, die
                                                        tomorrow if not sooner,
    And are both complainers.
Nuns are singing *Miserere*, as is only customary
    Over those in durance;
Tenor, mezzo, both are moaning; but above the sobs and groaning,
                                                        Leonora is intoning

Loving reassurance.
'If you will release my lover, Count, I'm ready to hand over,
    Breaking up this deadlock,
All I promised to Manrico; I will be your *beccafico* and your Golden
                                     Orange Pekoe
    In eternal wedlock!'
Manrico's free, but knows the price is pretty heavy, and the crisis
    Not imaginary.
Sure enough, his lady crying: 'I have taken poison!' flying to Manrico's
                                   arms, and dying,
    Needs the *Miserere*.
Di Luna finds himself unsuited, has Manrico executed;
    He has killed his brother!
Verdi's music's more compelling than this story I've been telling,
                          which ends with Azucena yelling
    She's avenged her mother!

PAUL GRIFFIN

——— RICHARD WAGNER ———

The Flying Dutchman

(*After Sir Henry Newbolt*)

It's the old *Flying Dutchman* and she's beating up the waves,
Though her crew are ghastly spectres who have left their wat'ry graves;

    And the lightning's flashing
    And the waves are crashing
    And the music's smashing,
      As the tempest raves.

It is eight bells ringing in a fishing port in Norway,
And Daland's daughter's singing as she stands within the doorway –

A-gazing at the picture with a pitiful emotion,
Of the doomed Dutch skipper who must ever roam the ocean,
For she loves him in her fashion with an all-transcending passion,
And would save him from his fate by her absolute devotion,

> And the lightning's flashing,
> And the waves are crashing
> And the music's smashing
> As the tempest raves.

He is doomed by a curse to roam the seas for ever
And nothing but a woman's love this Destiny can sever,
And once in Seven Years he's allowed to go ashore
To seek for the woman who will love him ever more,

> While the great sea crashes
> And the lightning flashes
> And the trombone clashes
> And the tempest raves.

He rewards Old Daland for a meeting with Senta
And he woos her in song with a voice like Stentor;
She falls, like a brick, for his power mesmeric
And deserts for the Dutchman her erstwhile Erik,

> While the waves are breaking
> And the backdrop's shaking
> And the oboe's faking
> The conductor raves.

Then it's he's off to sea in the storm and thunder
And it's she with a shriek that would split you asunder
Who dives from the cliff to be with him at last,
And the Curse is lifted, and down goes the mast!
And down goes the ship in the Deep Blue Sea,
And in Death their souls are united and free,
And light appears in the distant skies,

> While the strobes are flashing
> And the baton's lashing,
> And the music's smashing
> As the tempest dies.

It's the old *Flying Dutchman* and she sinks beneath the waves,
Her spectral crew, released at last, now seek their wat'ry graves,

> While the lightning's flashing
> And the tides are rushing
> And the usherette's ushing
> And the flautist's fretting
> And the leader's sweating
> And the front row's coughing
> And the critic's scoffing
> And the tabs are swagging
> And my verse is flagging
> As the tempest raves.

GERARD BENSON

Lohengrin

What ails her, poor Elsa? They've tarred her with murder;
    For nobbling her sibling she's reft of her realm:
This guerdon her guardian would gladly be gobbling,
    When up swims a swan with her swain at the helm.

What glamour to charm her! the glimmer of armour,
    The sweep of his sword as he swipes at the foe!
So shoddy old Freddy is battered and bettered
    And, Court-rid, with Ortrud to exile must go.

So bells are for Elsa — but bodeful the bridal:
    Anonymous still is her numinous knight;
While curious queries and spouses who needle
    Bring fatal requital — he cruises from sight.

The hatred of Ortrud — it prompted and tempted
    Unwary inquiry, and robbed her of joy.
She sobbed as he gave her an answer to grieve her:
    'Unmerciful Fate's lost you Parsifal's boy.'

O villainess, felonies soon will find nemesis:
    Feather a brother, then boast and be glad!
But Lohengrin will turn grins to horrified grimaces,
    Swapping his swan for that long-vanished lad.

While mortified Ortrud's swanupmanship's thwarted,
   With kisses his sis is revived – but we know,
When the boat is afloat and her *parti* departed,
   Preferred is the bird with a husband in tow.

MARY HOLTBY

Die Meistersinger von Nürnberg

Nuremberg's busy with musical jinks
But he who tries
To win a prize
Strict rules must follow,
Quite hard to swallow –
Worthwhile, so Walther thinks,
To win fair Eva as his bride.
His rival is Beckmesser,
Who's quick our hero to deride
When acting as assessor;
But Cobbler Sachs, a sage,
Predicts that Walt
Will end up all the rage.

Beckmesser's busy with musical jerks
But serenade
And Prize-song fade
Under the clamour
Of Sachs' loud hammer –
He gives the clerk the works.
Beckmesser then is glad to go,
Complete with Walther's lyric:
A victory which time will show
To be distinctly Pyrrhic.
But Cobbler Sachs, the wise,
Knows well that Walt
Will beat him for the prize.

Now comes the day
When all the people flock to hear

The contest for the prize.
Beckmesser's song offends the ear;
In disarray
Poor Walther's words appear, wrapped in bizarre disguise,
To meet with laughter . . .
But what comes after?
Walther stands up and sings:
His free, authentic song
Mounts up on angel-wings,
Entrancing all the throng
And lovely Eva claiming;
So, 'Master Singer' naming,
The judges give the prize.

MARY HOLTBY

Parsifal

Who'd be the Keeper of the Grail?
This holy man lies sick and pale –
Just for a moment, when seduced
His sacred spear from grip was loosed.
The wound inflicted by the spear
Won't heal, but from above we hear
That somebody can stop his pain –
A fool whose innocence is plain.

It's said that ignorance is bliss,
And none's so ignorant as this;
A vagabond who can't recall
His name, or anything at all.
This youthful, dumb, but guileless tramp
By accident comes in the camp
Of knights, but then gets pounced upon
For killing off their sacred swan.

It's obvious this witless fool
Has never even been to school,
But he somehow knows what's wrong and right,
And suddenly grows erudite

As, standing firm against temptation,
He avoids eternal condemnation.
He gets the sacred spear to cure
The weeping wound, remaining pure.

So all is well, at last, the broad
Who first seduced the Knight restored
To virtue (Parsifal released her).
It's all go for a Happy Easter.

KATIE MALLETT

DER RING DES NIEBELUNGEN

Das Rheingold

In the depths of the river the Rhine-maidens flit,
    Singing: 'Hello, old Alberich, hello!'
And an underground worker's the butt of their wit –
    He's a most disagreeable fellow.
From his lecherous grasp through the water they glide,
But a treasure of far greater worth he's espied:
It's the Gold – though its owner all love is denied,
    He carries it off with a bellow.

To the home of the gods we transport ourselves now,
    Singing: 'Hail, O Valhalla, Valhalla!'
Where the cost of fresh building's the cause of a row,
    With the threat of senescence and pallor.
For the Goddess of Youth is the price – but below
There's the gold for her ransom, so Wotan must go;
By a trick he extracts what he wants from his foe,
    Plus a curse as reward for his valour.

With the magical Helmet and Ring in his hoard,
    (But it's hollow, all hollow, all hollow)
His builders (two giants) he's out to defraud,
    An idea they're unwilling to swallow.
The curse starts to function – each fights for his share,
But if Fafner kills Fasolt, the gods do not care,

146

For in force to their palace in state they repair,
    Unaware of misfortunes to follow.

MARY HOLTBY

Die Walküre

Under a spreading forest tree
    The house of Hunding stands:
The host a hasty man is he
    And heavy with his hands;
It's pretty horrible to be
    Pursued by Hunding's bands.

But this is Siegmund's fate, who turns
    Up at his very door;
For Hunding's captive wife he yearns:
    It's mutual – furthermore,
Before the evening's passed he learns
    He's met the girl before.

While hubby settles for the night,
    Prepared at dawn to clash,
Sieglinde shows a sword stuck tight
    Into the sheltering ash;
To pull it out is Siegmund's right:
    He does – and then they dash.

Meanwhile, above, domestic strife
    Attends the gods' debate,
For Wotan gave the pair their life
    And longs to bless their fate;
But Fricka, Archetypal Wife,
    Upholds the married state.

So winged Brünnhilde, erst rehearsed
    Young Siegmund's life to save,
Is told: 'Let Hunding do his worst:
    His foe is for the grave.'
But rashly she prefers the first
    Instructions Wotan gave . . .

Alas! His spear, with fatal force,
    Shatters the ash-hewn sword;
This leaves poor Siegmund dead, of course,
    And poor Sieglinde floored;
But, hoisted on Brünnhilde's horse,
    To rally she's implored.

For since the lovely girl's in whelp,
    To cheer her up is vital.
Brünnhilde's sisters* aren't much help
    (*Valkyrie of the title);
They merely rush around and yelp,
    Awaiting crime's requital.

Yes – poor Brünnhilde's forced to pay
    By her impassioned sire;
He will not take her life away
    But lights an instant fire:
Inside its circle she must stay,
    Asleep where none can spy 'er.

Intruders won't disturb her kip,
    Unless Sieglinde's son
– If born – between the flames might slip . . .
    She clearly sees the fun
Involved in this relationship –
    A most peculiar one.

But what is it to us if aunts
    Their nephew would embrace?
And anyway, as yet the chance
    Is distant; slow the pace
Of unrelenting circumstance
    That shadows Wotan's race.

MARY HOLTBY

Siegfried

They call me MIME –
A crafty schemer;

148

And all my pleasure
    Is simply that:
Just for obtaining
The dragon's treasure,
I'm slyly training
    This awkward brat.

Nabbed as a baby,
It struck me, maybe
He'd grow a hero,
    Brave as his Pa –
Whose sword I'm trying
To weld, with zero
(I'm not denying)
    Result so far . . .

SIEGFRIED they call me –
Here all things gall me,
But most my 'father',
    That nasty gnome.
All that I'm seeing
Suggests that, rather,
Some higher Being
    Owes me a home.

He keeps on making
These swords – but breaking
Them up is easy –
    They're just no good.
Now hear him nag on:
'You should feel queasy;
This fearsome dragon
    Lives in our wood . . .'

They call me WOTAN:
My words denote an
Unpleasant fate for
    This coward here;
The sword's revival
A smith must wait for
Who bears no rival
    And knows no fear.

My own spear shattered
This bright blade – battered
And broke, to hamper
    A fateful strife.
Now Siegfried's sealed it
And now his Grandpa
Watches him wield it
    'Gainst Fafner's life . . .

SIEGFRIED in truth now,
No untried youth now
The blade I mended
    Has worked my will;
The woodbird's speech is
Now comprehended:
Mime, it teaches,
    Is next to kill.

Now free, unfettered,
Could life be bettered?
Yes – something jars me,
    I feel a lack . . .
Fresh paths I step on;
A spearman bars me;
I smash his weapon
    And drive him back.

A fiery circle –
What there may lurk'll
Be obvious if I
    Ride through the flame . . .
A soldier napping . . .
In just a jiffy,
His helmet tapping,
    I'll learn his name.

Her name's BRÜNNHILDE:
With love I've filled her,
She's bowled *me* over –
    We're both in shock.
The gold Ring's bound her
My faithful lover . . .

> At last I've found her,
>   My Queen of Rock.

MARY HOLTBY

Götterdämmerung

Tongues of fire intensely burning
Siegfried passed, all danger spurning;
Now for further fun he's yearning:
    Leaves his bridal bliss,
While the Gibichung are hatching
Complicated plots for matching
Gunther with Brünnhilde, catching
    Siegfried for their sis.
Nasty brother Hagen
Blinds them with his jargon –
Never said Brünnhilde's wed,
But claimed they'd get a bargain;
Mixed a love-inspiring potion:
Blithe Gutrune hailed the notion –
Now her heart is in commotion,
    Hot for Siegfried's kiss.

Yes, he's come – and tells his story:
Treasure trampled, dragon gory,
Helmet here to prove his glory
    (Girl has got the Ring).
Drinks all round – alas! no sooner
Has he quaffed the tainted schooner
Than he's daft about Gutrune;
    Can't recall a thing.
'Rocks a maiden lies on:
With the Helm's disguise on,
Will you o'erleap the fiery steep
For one *you've ne'er set eyes on?*
I can't see myself succeeding . . .'
'Splendid! Just the trip I'm needing!'
Brother-tie by mutual bleeding
    Seals their bargaining.

On the rocks the girl in question
Scorns her sister's wise suggestion:
Anyone with sense would best shun
  Rings that hold a curse.
As the bridal gold she's clenching
Enter Siegfried, quite unblenching,
Off her hand his love-gift wrenching –
  What a sad reverse!
Wedding preparation –
Signs of consternation:
Brünnhilde's mate inspires her hate
And bitter accusation.
Siegfried on a spearpoint swearing:
'Never gave the ring I'm wearing,'
Is undoubtedly preparing
  For a future hearse.

Spurned Brünnhilde's hopes fulfilling,
Hagen plots our hero's killing;
Plans a boar-hunt – Siegfried's willing,
  Glad as well to spend
Drink-time on his history dwelling;
Hagen's drug the truth compelling
Leaves him 'My Brünnhilde!' yelling
  As the blows descend.
Siegfried's dead – and shortly
Gunther's wounded mort'ly,
Who, keen to cling to Siegfried's Ring,
Finds Hagen quite uncourtly.
Into Siegfried's pyre his lover
Rides – the Maids the Ring recover,
Hagen gets a fatal shove (a
  Death no tears attend);
River Rhine to rest returning,
Curse expires – and we, discerning
That on high Valhalla's burning,
  Know we've reached the end.

MARY HOLTBY

Tannhäuser

You'd flaunt your faith in knightly pride?
Or double-cross the Cross in vice?
Throw Venus' grotto open wide?
Or stay as staid and chaste as ice?

Such queries we may not ignore:
Erotic dreams we entertain
May seal off Heaven's holy door.
So: SEX or SOUL? An old refrain.

We start this unctuous debate
By entering a randy den
Where nymphs and satyrs celebrate
Until too pooped to start again.

It's Venusberg, where sirens wail
And Tannhäuser, a carnal bard,
Is knackered. Body bruised and stale,
He feels his sin a mere charade.

He'll leave. But Venus, highly miffed,
Attempts dissuasion, so he names
The Virgin Mary (this can shift
The horniest of Venus' flames).

As Tannhäuser is deep in prayers
Upon the holy route to Rome,
Some former pals appear. How fares
The troubadour? He'll come back home?

His former sweet, serene, fair Liz
Is overjoyed at his return.
The minstrels' hall, she calls, is his.
And where's he been? She'd like to learn.

He flannels: 'Where Love holds all hearts';
She thinks this means a state of grace.
A minstrel competition starts,
And rival Wolfram takes his place.

The warblers sing of Love that's plain
Sublime, an otherworldly must,
But Tannhäuser, erotomane,
Eventually pipes up for lust.

A brawl ensues, and threats are rife
To mince the minstrel without fail.
It takes young Liz to save his life.
The deal? He'll hit the pilgrim trail.

The months fly by. Elizabeth
Awaits her songbird. Nothing's known.
She gets herself prepared for death,
While Wolfram, who's a baritone,

Implores the sacred Evening Star
To guide her feet to Heaven's Gate.
Here's Tannhäuser! A hip-hurrah?
Nein. He's in a shocking state.

The pope, it seems, was not impressed –
His staff, he said, would sooner bloom
Than save the soul of Venus' guest.
No wonder Tannhäuser's in gloom.

Barks Tannhäuser: 'The grotto, fast!'
Against this Wolfram vainly pleads,
But then young Liz, who's dead at last,
Though heaven-headed, intercedes.

It's Tannhäuser now kicks the can
As pilgrims bring the final laugh –
You know the pope who loathed the man?
Well, buds have blossomed on his staff.

What messages may we obtain?
That sensualists have little hope?
The only moral truly plain
Is: 'Never trust a pious pope.'

BILL GREENWELL

Tristan and Isolde

There's a famous seaside town in Cornwall
That's noted for jousting and fights,
And there, when the Ages were Darkest,
Dwelt Marke, in his court with his knights.

Young Tristan, a knight highly rated,
High-mettled and unknown to fear,
Had met, on a visit to Ireland,
Isolde, a maid without peer.

He's breathed to King Marke all about her:
Such beauty had seldom been seen.
The King said: 'All right, don't just stand there –
Go fetch her back here to be Queen.'

And that's how we meet the young fellow,
Aship where the Western winds blow,
With his binnacles, sextant and compass,
And Isolde stowed safely below.

Isolde, though, fancied him rotten;
She'd more room for knights than for kings.
An old man past sailing to fetch her
Might prove to be past other things.

She asked the lad down for a snifter,
But Brangäne, her maid, laced the brew
With passion-prone potions and philtres
Completely besotting the two.

King Marke claimed his bride, all unknowing,
But Tristan, now false, had no qualms
In twisting his genius to finding
His way to Isolde's warm arms.

They trusted a fellow called Melot,
Who took the King out for some sport,
But brought him straight back, without warning:
The pair *in flagrante* were caught.

The King just looked sad, but false Melot
Fell to gloating, the cheeky young pup,

So Tristan unsheathed and had at him –
But came away rather cut up.

King Marke, who was fond of his Tristan,
Decided his life-blood to spare,
And sent him instead into exile
On the ferry to Roscoff-*sur-Mer*.

In Brittany Tristan grew weaker;
The wound never seemed to congeal.
'Twas a psycho-so-matic condition
That only Isolde could heal.

Isolde was sent, and came running
(Or sailing, to tell the strict truth).
The sight of her sail on the skyline
Was the hope now sustaining the youth.

At last the ship came, and Isolde
Ran quickly to be by his side.
Pale Tristan, arising to greet her,
Regrettably fell down and died.

MORALS

It's wiser to mix your own cocktails;
Beware of a friend's double-cross;
And if secret amours are your weakness,
Steer clear of the wife of the boss.

NOEL PETTY

– CARL MARIA VON WEBER –

Der Freischütz

Carl Maria Friedrich Ernst von Weber
Led a life of most tremendous labour
Trying to write an opera not too tragical,
But noble, German, and distinctly magical.

Der Freischütz filled the bill; although it's grisly,
It mixes horror with a whiff of Bisley.
You can't translate the title, but, for fun,
I think of it as *Aennchen Get Your Gun.*

Agathe's a Bohemian girl who's mad
About the man who's working for her Dad,
Whose name is Max: he is a Forest Ranger,
A valiant chap, indifferent to danger
But much afflicted by one single thesis:
That all his marksmanship has gone to pieces –
Though why he needs to be a perfect shot
To marry Agathe, I have forgot.

Yet Max's fellow, Caspar, clever thing,
Can shoot an eagle when it's on the wing;
To Demon Samiel he's sold his soul;
In consequence the man can drill a hole
In any target, whether near or not;
He is what people call a demon shot.
'Come to Wolf's Glen,' he cries; 'don't be a goose!
We'll cast some magic bullets for your use.'

Meanwhile Agathe and her little cousin
Aennchen are singing twenty to the dozen.
Aennchen is cheerful, but Agathe's sad;
She fears her Max is going to the bad.
And here he comes; her fear's redoubled when
He tells her how he's heading for Wolf's Glen.
She knows it's a revolting little pit:
Imagine nastiness, then double it.

Now we are in the Glen: on rotting trees
Sit carrion crows, cawing in minor keys;
Phantoms of different kinds hover before us,
Muzak is coming from a spirit chorus;
Max sees a vision of his long-lost mother:
'Keep off the spells!' she cries. He doesn't bother.
Even Agathe's spirit has no force;
He goes ahead with Caspar on their course.

They cast seven magic shots – and with each one
Comes something horrid, like a skeleton;
But with the seventh Samiel alights –
The nastiest of all the nasty sights.
Yet Max is ready for the shooting test
And doesn't seem to care about the rest.
This all meets Caspar's hidden purpose: viz,
His partner's soul will go instead of his.

The morning of the test dawns sunnily;
The local Prince will act as referee.
The bride and maids are in their wedding frocks,
But do not laugh when Aennchen brings a box
Which causes Agathe to grit her teeth:
No bride's bouquet – instead, a funeral wreath.
Now starts the test, and Max does very well;
All goes as merry as a marriage bell.

The Prince points to a dove: 'Now pot that brute!'
'I am the dove,' cries Agathe; 'don't shoot!'
Too late: Max fires, and Agathe is downed;
But Caspar too has fallen to the ground.
The girl has only fainted. Caspar's struck;
She soon revives, but he is out of luck.
Max is repentant when he sees him fall,
And like a decent chap confesses all.

An ancient hermit suddenly emerges
Who understands about young people's urges
And picks up Agathe. He has been sent
By Heaven, to avert the Prince's banishment
Which justly is pronounced on Max's head.
'Be merciful!' he cries; 'sentence instead
This wretched Max to lead a married life.'
He does, and Agathe becomes a wife.

MORAL:

If you live in German forests
Be careful what you order from the florist's;

Keep off those spells, stick close to Heaven's law;
Don't try to be a Dangerous Dan McGraw.
Yet spurn all this, and Heaven won't let you down:
You still can wed the prettiest girl in town.

PAUL GRIFFIN

Oberon

You remember the silly old man
Who wrote verses that never would scan?
    When they asked why this was,
    He replied: 'It's because
I always like to cram as many words into my last line as I possibly
    can.'

When attempting an encapsulation
Of *Oberon*, Weber's creation,
    It was clear that the plot
    Would decidedly not
Lend itself to any verse treatment other than that employed in the silly
    old man's innovation.

The curtain comes up. All around
King Oberon's fairies abound.
    Puck appears on the scene
    Telling us that the Queen –
(Titania, that is) has quarrelled with the king who has vowed not to
    be reconciled to her until two constant lovers have been found.

Sir Huon, a knight of Bordeaux,
Has killed Charlemagne's son at a blow.
    The furious Dad
    Sends the lad to Baghdad
To slay whoever sits at the right hand of the Caliph and claim Reiza,
    the Caliph's beautiful daughter, as his bride – mind how you go!

So King Oberon makes up his mind
That he need go no further to find
    A loving pair who
    Might be faithful and true

Which would then allow him to give up his damnfool squabble with
    Titania since enforced celibacy does not agree with fairies. (We're still
    only in the middle of the first act and getting rather badly behind.)

(Apropos of the silly old man
Who wrote verses that never would scan . . .!
    It would seem that we must
    Very quickly adjust
The metre throughout the remaining verses in order to take account
    of the extremely complicated plot which Weber required his librettist
    to provide and to make a real effort to cram as much action into
    every LINE as we possibly can!)

Sir Huon and his squire Sherasmin, on their arrival in Persia, rescue
    Prince Babekan, the intended husband of Reiza, from a hungry lion
    but, had they known who he was at the time, they wouldn't have
    done.
Next day, at the court of Haroun el Rashid, it transpires that Babekan
    sits at the right hand of the Caliph; thereupon Sir Huon very
    properly slays him and elopes with Reiza who takes her maidservant,
    Fatima, along with her to join in the fun.
    Fatima has taken a fancy to Sherasmin, which he apparently
        reciprocates,
    And the two pairs of lovers make a determined dash for the palace
        gates

Where they are set upon by the guards but manage to beat them off
    with the aid of a magic horn. They are soon aboard a ship heading
    for a far country and are involved in the following further
    adventures while on the run.

(*Here 37 verses have been omitted,* Ed.)

    The tale ends in love-songs and laughter;
    All happily live ever after.
        The overture and
        The arias are grand . . .
    But could any libretto be dafter?

T. L. MCCARTHY

KURT WEILL

The Rise and Fall of the City of Mahagonny

Three vagabonds form a committee,
And set up a wide-open city;
    In flock the hookers,
    All jolly good lookers,
But Jenny's by far the most pretty.

Next to arrive on the scene
Are four lumberjacks, all of them keen
    To sample the action,
    And reach stupefaction
In every low dive and shebeen.

Jimmy, Jake, Bill, Joe – these four
Are soon offered floozies galore;
    But Jim chooses Jenny –
    He won't have just any
Attractive, available whore.

But soon disillusion sets in,
And some of the settlers begin
    To pay up and leave,
    And Jim's *joie de vivre*
Starts to ebb in this city of sin.

And now the bad news: a typhoon
Is due to hit town pretty soon;
    The panic's acute,
    But the storm changes route,
And everyone's over the moon.

Now the bacchanal's back at full blast!
And Jake has a mammoth repast:

Doing nothing by halves,
    He devours three whole calves,
And – still craving more – breathes his last.

A prize fight: Jim stakes all his bread
On Joe, but Joe ends up quite dead;
    Sighs Jim: 'RIP –
    The drinks are on me!'
But he's broke now, and deep in the red.

In that city, the only real crime
Is to not pay your bills in good time;
    Jim's tried by a sort
    Of kangaroo court,
And sentenced to die in his prime.

For Jim there is no passing bell,
As he bids Bill and Jenny farewell;
    In lieu of a will,
    He leaves Jenny to Bill,
And leaves them to rot there in hell.

RON RUBIN

The Threepenny Opera

Mackie Messer – Mack the Knife
Takes young Polly for his wife.
Mr Peachum, Polly's dad,
Is positively far from being glad.
Peachum runs a begging racket,
Making thus a pretty packet,
But wants Mack's pickings too, and shops
His new relation to the cops.
Chief Inspector Tiger Brown
Is not too keen to send Mack down,
For he and Mack are bosom friends,
And share their crooked dividends;
But Jenny Diver, Mack's old flame,

A glamour-puss who's on the game,
Turns him in – the rascal's jailed,
With not a hope of being bailed.

And now he's in another fix:
Forced to choose between two chicks –
Tiger's daughter Lucy, and
His wife (who Doesn't Understand),
He opts for Lucy – she's the blonde –
And Lucy helps him to abscond.
Now Peachum plans some aggravation:
He's going to wreck the Coronation
By rounding up each bum and vagrant,
Thus making London far from fragrant.
When Brown learns this he's most irate,
And goes to grab the reprobate;
'Why me? – get Mack!' old Peachum shouts:
'I know the scoundrel's whereabouts –
He's holed up with another whore!'
So Mack is nabbed and jailed once more.

Back in that old familiar cell,
Tiger calls to say farewell:
'They'll hang you, dear old pal!' he cries,
But – hold on, folks – Surprise! Surprise! –
The lucky blighter is reprieved,
And – this has got to be believed –
He gets a castle and a title –
A most astonishing requital . . .

MORAL

Though opera is a noble craft,
Most operatic plots are daft.

RON RUBIN

ERMANNO WOLF-FERRARI

Susannah's Secret

Cutting from Der Bavarische Tabakhandler, *Munich, 1910*

REVIEW: *SUSANNAH'S SECRET*

Herr Wolf-Ferrari's new work is quite enchanting. The plot is brief, witty and charming, and the melodies both memorable and eminently singable.

What is Susannah's secret? We would not wish to spoil the evening for you – you must go along and find out for yourself!

Warmly recommended.

Cutting from Deutsche Medizinische Tagebuch, *Munich, 1910*

REVIEW: *SUSANNAH'S SECRET*

The ludicrous plot of this festering piece of gutter-scraping can be summed up in a few tragic words:

Susannah, a secret smoker, marries a Count. Count smells tobacco, suspects infidelity, storms out. Susannah lights up, Count returns, reconciliation follows. Count takes up smoking.

In other words, infidelity = bad, smoking = good. Could anything be more irresponsible?

If Herr Wolf-Ferrari is really seeking to undermine everything the health education authorities have achieved over the past few years, he should stand up and say so. If not, he should remain *tacet*.

We will be demanding legislation to compel operatic companies not only to declare the identity of their sponsors (for we see the hand of commercial interests in this), but to print a Government health warning in every operatic programme.

NOEL PETTY

Interval Talk

*I like Wagner's music better than any other music. It is so
loud that one can talk the whole time without people hearing
what one says. That is a great advantage.*

Oscar Wilde (1854)

Wagner has beautiful moments but awful quarter hours.

Gioacchino Rossini

Arnold Bennett

Arnold Bennett to opera warmed
    And said: 'It is rightly called "grand" –
Provided, of course, it's performed
    In a language I don't understand!'

Voltaire

Should one have nothing else at all to do,
    Go to the opera, that's my suggestion,
Even although it may be only to
    Facilitate the process of digestion.

T. L. McCARTHY

Glyndebourne Interval

Overheard by a friend in the interval of *Der Rosenkavalier*.

'Well! Whose music is it, dear?'
'Mozart's, of course, dear.'
'MOZART! Are you sure?'
'Of course. All the music played here is by Mozart, dear. He built
    Glyndebourne for his wife, you know.'
'Well, then, he must have been very young. Before he learned how to
    write a proper tune.'

CICELY HERBERT

I've Got a Little List

As some day it may happen that a victim must be found,
I've got a little list – I've got a little list,
Of egregious opera-goers who might well be underground,
And who never would be missed – who never would be missed!
There's the scholar with his pocket-torch-illuminated score,
The parvenu who thinks his cash confers the right to jaw;
All ladies who, *de rigueur*, use their programme as a fan,
The 'modern' girls in ghastly clothes who think they're in a van;
All men who laugh too loud and long at esoteric jokes,
Incipient consumptives with their wheezes, coughs and chokes;
There's the millionaire from Texas with his awful wife and son,
Whose neck you'd like to twist – I've got him on the list;
And the noisy late arrivals pushing past you in Act One,
They never would be missed, they never would be missed.
There's the ostentatious critic who leaves halfway through Act Two,
Who cannot sing a note himself yet damns the ones who do;
The man behind informing you of what will happen next,
Who sighs aloud his pique at small excisions from the text;
And the fidget shifting endlessly from left to right and back,
Who during quieter moments likes to make his knuckles crack!
And the fop who *sotto voce* tries to play the humorist,
I know he'd not be missed – I know he'd not be missed.
The '*Encore!*' – yelling arriviste, that brash self-publicist,
All cheerers, weepers, booers, they'd none of them be missed;
And the teachers with their students, in decorum quite inept,
Who fail to check their charges by example or precept;
But it doesn't really matter who you put upon the list,
They'd none of them be missed, they'd none of them be missed!

TIM HOPKINS

Chorus Lines

(After practically any Gilbert & Sullivan opera)

We are the very pattern of a G & S Society,
Inheriting traditions of theatrical propriety,
We like to think that D'Oyly Carte, if he were looking down on us,
Would certainly approve our style and have no cause to frown on us,
But winds of change are blowing through our musical community,
From which not even G & S can dare to claim immunity;
We've got a new producer now who wants to change things drastically,
And some of us have welcomed him less than enthusiastically;
He says: 'Your style's outmoded – I can see I must correct a lot.'
(The man has very obviously been influenced by Brecht a lot).
He's revamped all the songs and claims he's substituted better words,
And to our consternation stuck in several four-letter words,
He'd like to do *The Gondoliers* on ice at Wembley Stadium,
And *Patience* with a topless chorus line at The Palladium,
He's ruled out *The Mikado* on the grounds that it is racial,
(It's making fun of differences linguistical and facial),
He plans a new production of another Savoy hardy 'un,
The Yeoman of the Guard will now become *The Avant Guardian*,
Poor *Princess Ida*'s been demoted from the aristocracy,
She's now just plain Ms Ida, in the interests of democracy,
He's re-done *Trial by Jury*, made it spicier and fancier,
The jury now gets nobbled by a Tokyo financier;
We asked him: 'What about *The Pirates, Iolanthe, Ruddigore*?'
The new man shook his head and said: 'No way. Not any bloody more.'
In short, the situation's now becoming quite Gilbertian,
Though if you dare to hint as much, the look you get's a dirty 'un.
Dismissing cavalierly all our repertoire encompasses,
With minimum delay he's caused a maximum of rumpuses.

He is the very pattern of those modern impresarios,
And we can only hold our breath and wait to see how far 'e goes.

STANLEY J. SHARPLESS

The Phantom of the Opera

(Book by Gaston Leroux)

My childhood years were rather grim,
Exposed to sermon, prayer and hymn;
No films or pantomimes or plays –
We shunned Satanic, worldly ways;
Of opera I'd not even heard,
Till Dad said: 'That's a Latin word.'

But then, at nine or ten I went
To Woolworth's with six pence and spent
It on a Readers' Library book,
Because I liked the jacket's look:
A corpse in velvet, deepest red,
With a plumed hat upon its head
Stalked slowly down a marble hall
And petrified the Opera Ball.

It caused me many a sleepless night,
But brought another world to light.
Sixty years on, I don't repent
A birthday sixpence so well spent!
I learned of *Faust*, the Jewel Song,
Of Marguerite, who went all wrong,
Of dancers who made brilliant matches
With mental noblemen – great catches –
Of boxes faced with gilded edges,
And *bonbonnières* on velvet ledges,
And, thanks to great Gaston Leroux,
I'm expert on the building too!

Twelve storeys high, baroque and grand,
The largest then in any land,
It was admired for style *and* sound –
The roof with domes and statues crowned,
And, throned upon a central spire,
Apollo with his gilded lyre.

The glorious foyer shone at night
With chandeliers ablaze with light,

And all the cream of Paris fashion
Met there for music, or from passion –
And ladies with camellias too
Made it their favourite *rendezvous*;
But while the lovers whispered prayers,
Or even listened to the airs,
How little did that audience know
Just what was going on below!

There were five cellar-storeys down,
Where dwelt a veritable town;
Fifteen horses for *Le Prophète*
Were stabled in the topmost set,
And in the four that lay below
Old rat-catchers went to and fro
To lure their Hamelin-hordes – but they
Looked far more evil than their prey.
Down there too was a treasure store,
Costumes, and scenery galore
Propped against walls, or hook or shelf;
There a scene-shifter hanged himself –
Or so they thought! They later found
That Someone Else lived underground.

Now every theatre has a ghost,
And this was rather worse than most,
So ugly that you'd never ask
To see him even *with* a mask;
He'd four black holes instead of features
And flesh that smelt like some dead creature's,
So could not go about the town,
But had to dwell four storeys down.
He saw well in the dark, and he
Enjoyed the best of music free.

One day this monster fell in love
With a young singer up above,
So he acquired a private box,
Ventriloquized, and gave folk shocks,
And, to advance his girl's career,
Brought down a giant chandelier.
Then, hoping she would be his wife
Snatched her off stage to share his life,

His lovely home down in the gloom,
The Louis-Philippe dining-room,
And all the comforts that were there –
Antimacassars on each chair,
An organ that he played all night,
The new-fangled electric light,
And central-heating there as well
To warm guests in the torture-cell,
And, round his house, a deep, dark mere,
Lest any rescuer should come near.

Though he tried all his charms upon her
He could not win his primadonna,
So threatened to blow up the place.
She compromised, and kissed his face.
If she hadn't, said Gaston Leroux,
Half Paris would have gone up too!
I am not French or musical, so
I think I'd rather have let them go!
But still, it worked. She got away;
The Opèra's still intact today,
And, too, the memory of its ghost,
A phantom feared – and loved – by most.
Film-makers owe much to Leroux,
And now Lloyd Webber's cashed in too.

O. BANFIELD

No Parsifal

(after Thomas Hood)

No Parsifal –
No thanks – no go – no way –
No inkling of the plot – no notion –
No time to catch the last bus home – no locomotion –
No alcoholic solace – no pubs stay open after –
No sex – no fun – no cheerfulness – no laughter –
No applause –
No wonder –

CICELY HERBERT

Why Opera is Popular

It used to be a class thing: enjoying opera once meant you had to have oodles of money, an Oxbridge education and a dress suit. But not any more. Opera, dammit, is becoming popular.

Sunday Express Magazine, 3 April 1988

The gangs of us that hang about
In velvet capes and cloaks
Aren't *bona fide* opera buffs:
We're incognito rocker roughs,
The sort of bullet-headed blokes
That like to bawl and shout.

Though loutish, we observe the scene,
Concealing cosh and gat.
You couldn't nobble us with cash,
Nor make our flash *machetes* slash
The punters with their opera chat,
No matter how they preen.

We mingle, mob within a mob,
And bob our heads with glee.
The swilling of a hundred gins,
Or shrieking of the violins,
We suffer enigmatically:
Because it is our job.

At home, a lager-can in hand,
We're *Iron Maiden* mad,
And throb to banshee bass guitar,
To drumbeat like an iron bar
Descending on a skull – we're bad
When beating in the band.

At work, *Der Rosenkavalier*
May make our stomachs churn;
It makes us nauseous and ill
To hear *The Barber of Seville*,
But we have got a crust to earn.
We are not there to hear.

We swan about at *Cav and Pag*,
We swell at Gounod's *Faust*.
Waltrud Meier, Rita Hunter –
These are names you'll hear us chunter,
And we remain polite, unsoused,
As mild as Melvyn Bragg.

We lead a '*Brava*!' for a diva,
Full of *bonhomie*.
We mention Offenbach, the Met,
We note the registers, and bet
That Kiri Te Kanawa's fee
Would baffle a believer.

We fill the stalls, we fill the gods,
We even stand in rain,
As when Domingo sang onscreen
At Covent Garden. What a scene!
Three thousand of us went insane,
And roared the tenor's odds.

We know the notes, the vital voice
(Anne Evans, Behrens, Pav);
At Glyndebourne, we arrive in hordes
And dress as marquises and lords,
And all of us possess the grav-
itas of Rolls and Royce.

Now some of you who come and go,
You Carlos Kleiber fans,
May well have noticed there are more
Attending opera than before;
Perhaps it has affected plans
You've made to see a show.

The bribery – its price is high?
The tickets – rarer yet?
Your right to wear your flashy frocks,
To purchase seats – perhaps a box –
Is not assumed. You have to sweat:
They're all in short supply.

And that's where we come in. You see,
The powers who lay down
How grants should be doled out, supplied,
And which cheap theatre group denied,
And who shall be the toast of Town,
Want opera subsidy.

What's hard about their sense of taste
To swallow, is its cost.
Your Wagner set will set you back;
The singer's pay is – well, top whack.
There's some who'd like them to get lost,
Think opera is *waste*.

But unemployment's off the graph
And we, who had no role,
Are now provided, free of tax,
Some fancy clothes to fit our backs,
Provided we're the life and soul
Of opera. Don't laugh –

They hire us to make a throng
So that the grant's maintained –
In fact, there's only fifty-six
Who go to witness vocal tricks,
Performed by singers finely trained
To warble foreign song.

This YOPeratic scheme, self-styled,
Is now for any age.
And any common girl or boy,
The proles, the oiks, the hoi-polloi,
Are guaranteed a steady wage,
That opera may run wild.

Now let us praise this living art,
Its arias, its grace,
The way that opera persists
Throughout the luscious, moody mists
Of time, and takes its rightful place
At British culture's heart.

BILL GREENWELL

The Pearl-flashers or *Simonna Boccanegra*

Fair face, in distant drama seen,
    The source of sumptuous trillings,
Avoid, I pray, the mini-screen,
    Where I can count your fillings.

MARY HOLTBY

The Idiocy of Opera

Music, when fat ladies die,
Why attempt to justify?
Odious are the chords that thicken
As the lass begins to sicken. . .

Rows of fools could go to bed
But choose to waste their funds instead;
And have they thought, when cash is gone,
Bluff is what it's squandered on?

MARY HOLTBY

The Castrati Clinic

'What we need,' mused Ukridge, 'is a Castrati Clinic. Terrific demand for them in opera, old boy. And once things get going, we could have our castrati in pop-groups, police-choirs; even singing leads in West End musicals. One could organize Castrati Eisteddfods, all over the country.'

'You don't mean,' whispered Bertie, recoiling in horror, 'that blokes will actually volunteer to have their what-have-yous, you-know-what, at your bally what's-its-name?'

'Put as succinctly as that, old fruit, yes. In a thriving market economy, there's no knowing what will sell, unless one actually tries it.'

Bertie paled at the thought. He tossed a largish gin down his throat.

'It's illegal, old man,' he wheezed, fixing a reproving eye on the entrepreneurial Ukridge.

'Can't see why,' declared Ukridge. 'It's a free country.'

'Not that free,' snorted Bertie, adding, 'Don't the fellows have to be rather young, before er ... I mean, haven't their thingimibobs got to be thingimijigged before their jolly voices thingimy?'

Ukridge's eyes gleamed.

'I'll do cut rates for the public schools. Probably touch the Arts Council for a thumping great grant ...'

'You'll be locked up,' predicted Bertie.

Ukridge paced the floor.

'If the authorities get a bit regimental about it, I'll probably push the boat out abroad ... Casablanca seems promising. Need a few pounds to put a prospectus together, though. I say, you couldn't lend me a tenner, could you?'

Bertie stepped back. His jaw dropped several inches in undisguised disdain.

'I'd ra...rather step under the proverbial omnibus, old sport,' he stammered.

Ukridge looked chastened. He stared down at his boots, miserably.

'All right, Bertie. You win. I won't do it.'

The Wooster countenance lit up like a Roman candle.

'Stout fellow,' he exulted, 'good egg. I always knew that you were basically sound, Ukridge.'

'Thank you for saving me from myself,' Ukridge sniffed.

RUSSELL LUCAS

Glyndebourne Intermezzo

Where Sussex Monteverdi dips
    Into the angle of a dream,
Some alien city slicker slips
    Strauss in his hair, and eyes the gleam
Of bright Rossini as he sips,
    And Mozart dancing on the stream.

MARY HOLTBY

We're Backing Britten

The stately opera-houses,
How beautiful they stand,
Traditional shrines of culture
In almost every land.

They cost a lot of money,
And never make ends meet,
Not even with full houses,
And bums on every seat.

But opera is good for you,
And it can reach the parts
(Big Business has discovered)
Unreached by other arts.

It's good Public Relations –
A tax-avoidance wheeze –
To bale out Covent Garden
With hefty subsidies.

To say opera's élitist
Is just a load of gammon;
Put P R into oPeRa
And please both God and Mammon.

STANLEY J. SHARPLESS

A Ballade of Opera-going

No opera lover's prepared to admit
What ought to be clear to them all:
That it's not the libretto that makes for a hit
But the way that a diva can bawl.
When Freni or Norman can fill a large hall,
Singing lines that are more or less rot
About Orpheus, Mars, or Amadis of Gaul,
It's the music that matters – to Hell with the plot.

The price that is asked for a place in the pit,
That's described as an orchestra-stall,
Is enough to give any accountant a fit;
And the bar is far-distant and small.
If you can't see the stage because you aren't tall,
If you're crowded and fearfully hot,
Don't forget, as you long for the curtain to fall,
It's the music that matters – to Hell with the plot.

Monteverdi, or Wagner, or Benjamin Britt,
Would agree, being pushed to the wall,
That the words and their meaning don't matter a bit,
For who, unless gifted with total recall,
Can remember the story of Verdi's *Masked Ball*,
Or Puccini's Chinese *Turandot*,
Or *Don Juan* that ends with a furious brawl?
It's the music that matters – to Hell with the plot.

Envoi
Prince, when at the Garden you lounge in your stall,
On expenses, as likely as not,
Remember the maxim that justifies all,
It's the music that matters – to Hell with the plot.

JOHN STANLEY SWEETMAN

Hamlet

(*Humphrey Searle's opera* Hamlet *was first produced at Covent Garden and abandoned after one and a half performances.*)

When Shakespeare's text was set by Searle
The Garden gave his work a whirl;
But after rehearsing for weeks and weeks
The Prince himself eschewed its shrieks,
And thus it was that few would see
An opera destined not to be.

CICELY HERBERT

Cav and Pag

Cav and *Pag*, *Cav* and *Pag*,
They go together like zig and zag;
They've never been billed as *Pag* and *Cav* –
I wonder why they never have?
The reason why, I think I twig,
It'd sound as silly as zag and zig.

STANLEY J. SHARPLESS

The Plots Thicken

(*A Mini-Ballade*)

The British have done very well for Pacini,
For whom Abbotsford was a major resource.
Likewise Donizetti, Bizet and Bellini;
All borrowed Scott's tales with no hint of remorse.
Was Byron alive would he ever endorse,
Say, Verdi's *Foscari*, I rather think not.
So, for first-class romances it's par for the course
That you'll find them in Byron, or Shakespeare, or Scott.

Othello's served Verdi and also Rossini;
There are thirty-odd *Tempest*s and real *tours de force*.
The Shrew fed Cole Porter and, after, Giannini;
Old Falstaff's career is a constant recourse.
If a heroine's fate is not death but much worse,
When a character's strangled, or poisoned, or shot;
Just remember the author and mutter: 'Of course.
I read this in Byron, or Shakespeare, or Scott.'

Envoi
Prince, if you should venture to look for the source
Of a story, the bones of an opera's plot,
It appears to be almost a matter of course,
That you'll find it in Byron, or Shakespeare, or Scott.

JOHN STANLEY SWEETMAN

180

Opera People

I liked your opera. I think I will set it to music.
> Ludwig van Beethoven

Wagner's music is better than it sounds.
> Mark Twain

What! All this for a song?
> Queen Elizabeth I

John McCormack (1884 – 1945)

His diction and phrasing
Were fine beyond praising,
His timbre a purist's delight,
But the critical clique
Said his acting was weak,
And he knew in his heart they were right –

So forsaking the stage
He became all the rage
As a very high-class balladeer,
His repertoire rich
With a mixture of Kitsch
And the gems of his opera career –

Some thought this poor taste
And a trifle two-faced,
Forgetting that one of his goals
Was to ravish with song
A disparate throng
Of the highbrows, the mods and the proles.

PHILIP A. NICHOLSON

Lost Luggage

In opera in days long gone
There was this odd phenomenon
Of men who sang in treble voice,
Shorn of two reasons to rejoice;
Your golden-voiced young chorister,
Nabbed by some choral connoisseur,
Was flogged to barbers he employs
To poach the eggs of altar boys.

Society, by prelates led,
Gave this abuse the go-ahead,
And clerics even had the gall
To put the blame upon St Paul,
Who (if Corinthians you search)
Said women should keep *stumm* in church,
Which thus implied (they said) in choir,
If stronger treble you desire
To sing *fortissimo* full pelt,
He absolutely must be gelt;
(Since 1680 there've been plenty –
The last survived till 1920) –
Thus, as Castrato, he can bat
Right up to c♯ from b♭
From vocal cords of boyish span
And lung-power of a full-grown man.
In voice that fills great concert halls,
Each rich soprano note enthrals,
But though when he on stage performs
Excited ladies swoon in swarms,
When they take him home (to tea)
It's quite another ball-game; he,
Faced by Milady tête-à-tête,
Alack can't set the record straight
Where in his lower register
Amplification she'd prefer.
So soon she says she cannot stand
The fellow; he's a dead loss, and

However hard a bird may search,
On him she'll never find a perch;
And thus discarded, he decides
That Fame and Fortune be his guides,
Plays hard to get, bumps up his fees,
Throws tantrums nothing can appease,
Retires, estate and title buys,
And who can blame his enterprise –
Poor chap, of substance though so great,
He's always two stones underweight.

W.F.N. WATSON

Two Clerihews

Boris Christoff
Was pretty pissed off
When somebody called him a vulgar
Bulgar.

Pavarotti
Drives women potty,
But, although they hound him,
They find it hard to get round him.

RON RUBIN

Carmen

When Georges Bizet produced his *tour de force*
(Reckoned a failure at the time, of course)
In eighteen fifty-five, few would have guessed
How all the wide world would become obsessed
With Gypsy maiden Carmen and her lovers;
How, when Don José the dragoon, discovers
Her crush on Escamillo, mutters: 'Charming!'
Pulls out a knife and carries on alarming . . .
The fever duly led to the creation
Of fresh productions throughout every nation.
Carmen set everywhere but in Iberia –
In Nicaragua, Norway and Nigeria –
Carmen in Yiddish, Dutch and Esperanto –
Carmen in hard rock – *Carmen* as panto.
Carmen on ice – *Carmen* on roller skates –
Carmen, in China, busy juggling plates.
Carmen in drag and *Carmen* in cross-dress –
A kilted *Carmen*, venue Perth, no less.
C. B. de Mille's first *Carmen* on the screen,
In which a host of singing stars were seen,
All lured to Hollywood at vast expense
To make a *silent* film. (Now *that* makes sense?)
The all-black *Carmen Jones* in New York alleys
(And not a mining village in the Valleys!)
And *Carmen* yellow, pinko-white and red . . .
(*That will be quite sufficient* Carmens, Ed.)
They tell us that a whizz-kid in Korea
Has hit upon a really fresh idea –
A brand-new *Carmen*, set in Old Seville
In eighteen twenty-one – production will
Be based along the lines Bizet devised
And not a whit revised or modernized.
(It's due to open next year at the Met.)
Good God! How *avant-garde* can people get?

T. L. MCCARTHY

186

Farinelli

In Italy, three hundred years ago,
It was the custom, if a boy should show
Great purity of vocal tone and range,
To make quite sure these features would not change.
Thus, if the lad was of a humble station,
He would be given A Certain Operation,
His father gaining ample recompense,
Leaving the youth to bear the consequence.

Whether young Carlo Broschi got his lesions
For medical or mercenary reasons
We cannot know; but when, at age fifteen,
He burst upon the operatic scene,
His fame spread far beyond his Naples home,
And two years later he appeared in Rome.
By now, he had an eye to wider fame
And Farinelli seemed a better name;
In opera, as in a later day,
A fancy name might get you half the way.

It was in Rome that Mr Burney wrote
The famous tale of Farinelli's Note:
An aria sung by the great castrato,
Accompanied by trumpet obbligato,
Became a contest of which one was stronger –
Who could keep up the twirls and twiddles longer.
Eventually the trumpeter expired
Whereon our hero, jubilant and fired
By this subdual, shook and swelled the note
And held it in a long triumphant gloat.
The audience went wild with one accord
And Farinelli's fame was blazed abroad.
In Italy, they have a long tradition
Of opera-as-athletic-competition.

Eventually, in 1734,
He landed on a waiting England's shore,
Invited to endorse with his ability
The new-formed Opera of the Nobility,

A venture got up by the upper classes
To do down Mr Handel and the masses.
He stayed three years, enjoying adulation
From every section of the population.
Fine gentlefolks were shunned, had they not each
Heard Farinelli sing and Foster preach.
One fashionable dame was heard to utter:
'One God, one Farinelli!' in a flutter.
On top of his two thousand guinea salary,
Liberal pensions from his ducal gallery
Descended on him like autumnal hails,
A habit started by the Prince of Wales;
And few there were indeed who did not grieve
When Farinelli was induced to leave.

Philip the Fifth of Spain was far from jolly;
In fact, he was so prone to melancholy
His dauntless Queen, Elizabeth Farnese,
Desperate to stop the old man going crazy,
(For if he were to do so, it would mean
She'd surely have to give up being Queen)
Hired Farinelli at immense expense
To see if music could induce some sense.
She kept him up her sleeve, then one black day
Unleashed The Voice from several rooms away.
It did the trick: the King was filled with awe,
Regained his wits, and reigned for nine years more.
Poor Farinelli through those nine long years
Nightly reduced the King to happy tears
With four sweet arias from his peerless voice.
The same four: Philip never changed his choice.

So massive was his influence at court
His wisdom and sagacity were sought
On various schemes of drainage, irrigation,
Matters of imports, exports and taxation.
Thus by a curious, random trick of fate
The star became a minister of state,
And, higher honour still, Commendador,
Which none but noblemen had won before.

And so, a voice with power to enthral
Which started with th'unkindest cut of all
Brought Farinelli glory and repute;
Which leaves one question as distinctly moot –
As oft in life, his fortune had a cost:
Was what he profited worth what he lost?

NOEL PETTY

Two More Clerihews

The voice of Dame Janet
Is out of this planet;
Nothing is so harrowing
As to hear her *Che Faro*-ing.

Pavarotti
Drives Carnegie Hall quite potty;
It's me that's cranky,
But I wish he could do it without the hanky.

NOEL PETTY

Amelita Galli-Curci (1882 – 1963)

A Clerihew

To Galli-Curci's 'Lo hear the gentle lark!'
Many a listener would hark:
But I doubt if her trilling
Ever made a lady lark more willing.

MARGARET ROGERS

The Cautionary Tale of Jean-Baptiste Lully (1632–1687)

(Who not so much Put his Foot in It as Put It in his Foot)

This is the Tale of Jean-Baptiste,
A touchy, volatile Artiste.
In Italy, where he was raised,
The Little Fellow's skill amazed
A Holidaying Chevalier
Who bagged him as a souvenir.
His Prowess on the Violin
Put French musicians in a Spin;
His delicacy in the Dance
Was famed the Length and Breadth of France.
All this, plus flattery warm and gooey,
Endeared him to the Fourteenth Louis.
Advancement thus came Swift and Sure,
And Operas followed, score on score.
Phaëton, Atys and *Armide*
Supplied the King's insatiate greed.
But Jean-Baptiste was greedy too,
Demanding More than was his Due,
Including that most grasping Fee,
An Opera Monopoly.
No Rival could his work present
Except with his express consent;
If some new Talent should appear,
He'd stamp his foot and cry: 'Not here!'
He thus became securely based
With Money, Houses, and a Taste
For Unimaginable Vice –
He really wasn't very nice.

Conductors then would wield a stick
Some five feet long and fairly thick
To thump the Time out; and one day,
Conducting in his haughty way
The Royal Band, Jean-Baptiste put
The Baton right into his foot.

Whether the Orchestra applauded
Is mercifully not recorded,
But soon Infection took its hold
And Jean-Baptiste was Stiff and Cold.

MORAL

Your Music may be Quite Delightful,
But that's No Reason to be Spiteful.

NOEL PETTY

Two Views of Richard Wagner

Self-Praise

My name is Richard Wagner, I'm
    An operatic paradigm;
My genius is plain to see,
    All rivals must defer to me.
I cannot work with lesser men;
    I write my own librettos when
It's clear that no one understands
    The miracles my Muse demands.

No Recommendation

The music is magnificent,
    The words alas, 'so-so';
The man himself is not I fear
    Very nice to know.
His interests outside opera
    Are the mad pursuit of pelf
And a passionate involvement
    With his overweening self.

PHILIP A. NICHOLSON

191

Duet

GILBERT & SULLIVAN: To some we may seem
      As quite indivisible.
    { His
      My } melody's wed
  To { his
       my } verses so risible;
  But when matters came
      To financial legality
  We each had our own
      Perverse personality.

GILBERT: A carpet it was
      Divided our loyalties;
  Why on earth should it come
      Out of *my* hard-earned royalties?
  This stemmed up the flow
      From our rich cornucopia,
  So a *Limited*'s tagged
      To my next one – *Utopia*.

SULLIVAN: That lozenge of his,
      Resurrected persistently!
  How could I react
      Otherwise than so distantly?
  My muse could not stoop
      To such silly vulgarity,
  Though *The Yeomen* deserves
      Its distinct popularity.

GILBERT & SULLIVAN: O let us not dwell
      On these unpleasant quarrellings
  For time has bestowed
      Us our knighthoods and laurellings.
  It's true that we have
      No bearings armorial,
  But each one may boast
      An Embankment Memorial!

JOYCE JOHNSON

Operatic Limericks

An opera lover called Healey
Once put on *The Ring* in Swahili
  The natives of Hull
  Found it all rather dull,
As did the good burghers of Ely.

Said Handel: 'Please don't call me Herr,
I'm really quite British – so there!
  And please, ven I croak
  I vould like (vot a joke!)
A coffin marked "Handel With Care".'

On Verdi, Giuseppe, I'm keen;
His name (if you know what I mean)
  Quite rolls off the tongue –
  It can almost be sung –
A pity it just means Joe Green.

A keen Wagner fan is our Geoff,
Especially when played triple *f*;
  'Some folks find him hellish,'
  Says Geoff, 'but I relish
The noise, as I'm almost stone-deaf.'

An opera singer called Mae
Sang *Carmen* in Haifa one day;
  The audience booed her,
  And a critic reviewed her
In two little words, viz: '*Oy veh!*'

RON RUBIN

The Art of Embroidery

Rossini was heard to remark: 'It's quite hellish
How divas with devilish relish embellish
The Pieces that take me so long to compose.
It's gilding the lily to superimpose
Such vocal gymnastics, runs, roulades and trills,
On tunes which, quite patently, need no such frills!'
Rehearsing his *Barber* with Patti one day,
She ad-libbed the air, in her usual way –
'*Una voce* (*tra-la!*) – *poco fa* (*yoo-hoo-hoo!*)'
(The coloratura at Act one, Scene two.)
The Maestro, apparently, heard her out placidly,
Then turned to the singer and questioned her acidly:
'There's one point I'd like to clear up, if I may;
Who composed, Adelina, that aria, pray?'

                                        T.L. MCCARTHY

Some Sopranos

MARIA MALIBRAN (1808 – 1836)
They say Maria Malibran
Was rather partial to a can
Of foaming ale – or three or four –
Or maybe, on occasion, more.
She died at twenty-eight, poor dear.
(We think we know that brand of beer!)

ADELINA PATTI (1843 – 1919)
The impresario's face fell
When Patti specified her fee.
'How many thousand dollars, hell!
That's real exorbitant,' said he.
'Perhaps I should make one thing clear:
I just want you to sing, my dear!'

DAME NELLIE MELBA (1861 – 1931)
'Just sing 'em muck,' Dame Nellie cried,
'That's all the bastards understand,'
When someone asked her to provide
A programme for her native land.
They still hate Melba's guts for that
In Bendigo and Ballarat.

LUISA TETRAZZINI (1871 – 1940)
Luisa used to pick up guys
Obsessively – she liked 'em tall;
But even guys of lesser size
Were better than no guys at all.
She ate spaghetti day and night
To sharpen up her appetite . . .

MARIA CALLAS (1923 – 1977)
Maria Callas asked for such
A vast fee in the USA . . .
'We don't pay presidents that much,'
Sir Rudolph Bing was heard to say.
Callas replied: 'Is that so, Bing?
Well, get the president to sing!'

T.L. MCCARTHY

More Clerihews Yet

Maria Callas
Never watched *Dallas*;
She'd much rather curl up with a hot-water bottle
And Aristotle.

When Kirsten Flagstad was stung
In the Middle of *Götterdämmerung*;
She cried: 'Drat',
And hit a bee flat.

RON RUBIN

Tops

A Maestro to a Promising Young Singer
(After Cole Porter)

You're the tops!
You are Pavarotti.
You're the tops!
You are Kurt Weill's Lotte.
You're a Mozart tune, Glyndebourne in June, Purcell;
You're *The Gondoliers*, you're Peter Pears, Maurice Ravel.

You're the tops!
You're *Il Trovatore*.
You're the tops!
You're *L'elisir d'amore*
You are *Peter Grimes*, Gilbertian rhymes, Bartók;
You're *Salome*, Jules Massenet, *The Golden Cock*.

You're the tops!
You are *Rigoletto*.
You're the tops!
You're a Brecht libretto.
You're a *diva* that is not too fat or thin;
You're Berg's *Wozzeck*, you're Janáček, you're *Lohengrin*.

You're the tops!
You're Milan's *La Scala*.
You're the tops!
You're *Das Lied* of Mahler.
You are *Figaro, Manon Lescaut, Carmen* –
Now, baby, sing that aria ONCE AGAIN!

MARGARET ROGERS

More Operatic Limericks

There was an old bass called d'Amato,
Who sang quite *appassionato*;
    We all shed a tear
    When he fell on his spear,
But he's now quite a well-known castrato.

An Athenian singer called Nina
Was partial, it seems, to Retsina;
    She's been all the rage
    Since she staggered on stage,
And stripped to a slow cavatina.

An androgynous chappie called Peake
Had a range which was surely unique;
    He sang bass and contralto,
    Soprano and alto,
But his treble was more like a shriek.

*A tenor who hailed from Lepanto
Was known for his splendid *bel canto*;
    But as for his *lieder*,
    His German, dear reader,
Was rather like bad Esperanto.

There once was a great prima donna,
Whose co-star leaped madly upon her;
    'Let's make it!' he cried.
    'Sure thing,' she replied,
'But right here onstage I don't wanna!'

RON RUBIN

* From *'88 Musical Limericks* pub. by Useful Music.

Metastasio, the Great Librettist

Great Metastasio in his youthful time, his youthful time, his youthful
  time, his youthful time
Showed mastery at improvising rhyme, showed mastery, showed mastery,
  showed mastery, showed mastery at improvising rhyme,
Which led to his adoption, his adoption, which led to his adoption by a
  gent
Who later died, who died, who later died and left him every cent, left every
  cent.
His opera, his opera libretti were the rage
With every great composer, great composer of the age.
His opera, his opera libretti were the rage
With every great composer, great composer of the age,
Including Handel, Haydn, Gluck and Mozart,
Yes Handel! And Haydn! And Gluck! and Mozart!
Including Handel, Haydn, Gluck and Mozart,
Whose august testimonial denotes Art,
Denotes Art, denotes Art,
With Haydn, Gluck and Mozart.
The audience thus knew his words right off, they knew, they knew his
  words right off, right off,
Which helps a lot, which helps a lot when people start to cough, yes start
  to cough, yes start to cough,
Cough! Cough!

NOEL PETTY

Opera Places

COVENT GARDEN

Sir, we are a nest of singing

Sir, we are a nest of singing birds.

Dr Samuel Johnson

Writ from the Heart by the Principal Clarinet of ROH

Though clarinet and bold bassoon
Believe that they convey the tune,
Their efforts o'er the radio
Are drowned by Don Ottavio.

IAN HERBERT

The Good Old Days

THE COLISEUM (home of English National Opera, originally a variety theatre) (After Francis Thompson)

It is little I repair to the opera in English,
Though it's the only language that I know,
It is little I repair to the opera in English,
For I'm thinking of another kind of show;
The theatre's full of shades, from gallery to stalls,
And there are ghostly echoes from the old-time music-halls
And I look through my tears as they take their curtain calls,
  As the scene-shifters flicker to and fro
    At ENO –
O my Robey and my Formby long ago!

STANLEY J. SHARPLESS

Bayreuth Festival Theatre

Ludwig was quite gone on Richard!
Would you know how it came out?
In cartoons, captioned, were they strictured –
Some High German, some Low Kraut!
Now, Ludwig was a Bayreuth dandy,
And, some thought, a doting King,
While Richard, short, but no-way bandy,
Just wanted to promote *Der Ring*!

'On that hill,' cried Ludwig, warming,
'I shall raise an opera house,
With chaise-longues and Rembrandts swarming,
In tune with our German *nous*!
Wan, wee-statured, raptured Wagner,
I can build a place so posh,
Just to house your *Opus Magner*,
That will dwarf *Rathaus*, or *Schloss*!'
Critics, Dons, (tons) maids and matrons,
To our PR Lunch we'll bring!
(Though Tchaikovsky's hunch proved patrons
Preferred cutlets to *The Ring*!)

'Now we're into building, would you
Do a villa for old Dick?
I'm so hard-up, Ludwig, could you?
I've exhausted all my tick!'
Well, despite a Grand Beginning,
Bayreuth soon goes in the red,
So Richard – how can one help grinning –
Does it on the rates, instead!
Now, gold stair-rods they are buying;
Staff retiring-rooms abound.
Repertoire with red-tape vying,
New Bayreuth gets off the ground!

When the gentry, in plush seats, now,
Asked how it was done so slick,
Ludwig, proud of German know-how,
Answered: 'VORSPRUNG DURCH TECHNIK!'

Richard, though still short on 'oncers',
Then writes *Parsifal*; has tea!
Gives the franchise to his sponsors –
BAYREUTH (Bayern) UDC!

PASCOE POLGLAZE

The Royal Opera House, Covent Garden

An extract from: Rings and Things – *The Story of Opera for boys and girls by H. E. Marshall, author of* Our Island Story.

The noble Knights who run the Royal Opera are very kind-hearted because they give em-ploy-ment to thousands of people. These people all work very hard to amuse THE AUDIENCE. THE AUDIENCE is made up of people who don't have to work. That is why operas go on for hours and hours and hours. The very rich people who don't have to work can lie in bed the next day and read what THE CRITIC thinks about the opera. Alas! THE CRITIC is usually a person who doesn't like opera and e-special-ly doesn't like the people who work at Covent Garden. One cruel man called THOMAS NUTCLIFFE is always very cross about THE BAND. The grown-up name for THE BAND is THE ORCHESTRA. Now, the men in THE ORCHESTRA are rather babyish. That is why there are one or two ladies in THE ORCHESTRA. The ladies en-courage the babyish men to change their socks some-times and not to make rude noises in the quiet bits. THE CONDUCTOR is in charge of the music and is prob-ably a bit like your governess with a big stick. It is lucky he is too busy to hear the words and the conductor would be very sur-prised and shocked if he could understand Rugby songs, but luckily he can't be-cause he is foreign. All members of THE CHORUS are Welsh and they are very happy people be-cause there is lots of time in between choruses to go to the bar and have a drink.

CICELY HERBERT

L'Arena, Verona

A popular place is Verona,
With Roman remains by the ton,
And so Mr and Mrs Ramsbottom
Came here, with young Albert, their son.

A bright little chap were young Albert,
Who'd studied the Romans in class,
And knew all about Nero and Caesar,
And thought Claudius a bit of an ass.

He'd a special attachment to lions
(For reasons too long to relate)
And the Romans, he knew, fed 'em Christians
In some games, on a specified date.

'It's much further than Blackpool,' thought Father,
'But it's nice to encourage the lad
To show off all this fine education,
And make use of the schooling 'e's 'ad.'

It was Rome Albert wanted to stay in,
But hotels there were all out on strike,
So their agent had said: 'Try Verona.
All Italian towns is alike.'

'T were near dark when the aeroplane landed,
So Mrs Ramsbottom said: 'Bed!'
But young Albert begged hard to go walking
And his father said: 'Ee! Go ahead!'

On his map Albert found The Arena,
Where he'd thought that the lions might be;
So they went, just to look, before bedtime,
To see if there's owt there to see.

There were lights and big crowds round the gateways,
'There's a show!' said young Albert with glee.
And his father said: 'Don't get excited,'
And Mother had said: 'Not for me!'

But young Albert was pushing and shoving,
He wanted to have a good seat;
So they got themselves in, on the terrace,
Where the stone was still warm from the heat.

'It'll set off your piles,' warned his mother,
As Albert sat craning his neck.
'I can't see no lions,' he whimpered.
Mother said: 'It's a bit of a wreck.

'Make a nice lot of work for some builder.
There's no plaster at all on them walls.'
But Father said: 'Nay, don't tha' panic.
We're insured in case anything falls.'

'I 'ope they've got plenty of Christians,'
Said Albert aloud: 'There's the band.
It's just like the sea-front at Morecambe,
And they're playing right loud – this is grand!'

But no lions came out on the platform,
Only women in long fancy dress.
And the band played on, louder and louder,
Father said: 'I *am* vexed – what a mess!'

Albert shouted: 'Come on with them lions!'
And the crowd cried: '*Silenzio!*' (Shut up!);
So Albert blew out all their candles
Which caused them to get right cut up.

On the stage they were singing a chorus;
Albert started to cry and to scoff.
He said: 'We've been 'ad – there's no lions,
Or Christians, or blood. So I'm off.'

'You'd 'ave thought they'd stick to tradition,
And be proud of their long 'istory.
What! spend all me time 'earing music
Wi' no lions, no Christians! Not me!'

D. A. PRINCE

A Visit to Glyndebourne

(After John Betjeman)

Let me get my evening suit out,
Is it fit for Glyndebourne stalls?
Ages since I saw an opera,
(*Traviata*, one recalls).

Two free tickets for your birthday,
Nice idea of Auntie Pat's,
Must be careful not to let on
That we'd rather have seen *Cats*.

Don't forget the opera glasses,
I must take my hearing aid,
Though the whole thing's in Italian,
Quite beyond me, I'm afraid.

Still, the programme will explain it,
With an outline of the plot,
(Incidentally, is it silent –
That last 't' in *Turandot*?)

Fortnum's do a picnic basket
With some rather scrumptious food.
Salmon, caviare and champers
Help to put one in the mood

For the summer lawns of Glyndebourne,
Sort of Ascot in its way,
Standing for the good old values
In the punk world of today.

There's a fast train from Victoria,
Saves a long drive – such a boon,
Though one does feel rather silly,
Dinner-jacketed at noon.

Does one clap after each aria?
Best to see what others do;
Hope it won't go on too long, dear,
Last train back – 10.42.

STANLEY J. SHARPLESS

Snape Maltings

If you're staying near Snape
You cannot escape
The music that's made at the Maltings;
It drifts through the rushes
And tangles in bushes
And swirls round the edge of the saltings.
From Bombay or Bahia
Murray Perahia
Flies in, and has everyone listening;
Rostropovitch, called 'Slav'
Because no one will have
A shot at the name of his christening,
Arrives with his cello –
A lovely old fellow
Who trains up a packet of pupils;
But when we all learn
It's the opera's turn
The local excitement quadruples.
For all through those years
When Britten and Pears
Were alive and in charge of the tiller
English opera's been
At the centre of scene
As an auditorium filler.
So, instead of complaining
That opera's waning,
You'll climb in a train if you're clever,
And think in your carriage
Of *The Midsummer Marriage*
Or *The Turn of the Screw* or whatever.
And should you arrive
At the Maltings alive
(British Rail, I am told, is improving),
When you hear the first snippet
Of Britten or Tippett,
I doubt if you'll want to be moving.

PAUL GRIFFIN

La Scala

(*Tune* 'O Sole Mio')

Oh, great La Scala
Of Italy,
The home of tuneful loquacity,
Two hundred years you've been the site
Of many an on and off stage fight.

Though here Rossini
Made a debut,
Bellini, Verdi, Puccini too,
Once Toscanini put down his foot
To make a closing night kaput.

When all of Europe
Went off to war
Though you stayed put you knew the score.
A sitting target and bombs quite soon
Brought down the house, without a tune.

When Mussolini
Tried to impose
A fascist anthem on first night shows
You stood your ground in the dispute
To give the Nazi stamp the boot.

Here gambling flourished
For raising cash,
Though the producers weren't quite so rash –
No boos or catcalls were allowed –
For Italy, a sober crowd.

Oh, great La Scala,
With a high scream
Maria Callas here let off steam
To patrons perched around the stage
Like lovebirds in a gilded cage.

With Zeffirelli
To fan the flame
On film and telly you've global fame.
When I can't go to Italy
Let video bring it to me!

KATIE MALLETT

Tommy's View of Glyndebourne

(After Rudyard Kipling)

For music wot is serious, in a country-'ouse wot's jolly,
The 'ighbrow opera-lovers wiv a fair amount o' lolly
Come dahn each year to Glyndebourne – and it really beats the band,
'Cos the opera's in a lingo few of 'em can understand.

Oh it's Cozy Fanny Tooty *every season, by request,*
But it's "Knocked 'Em In The Old Kent Road" that Tommy loves the best.

They sits there gawpin' in the stalls, like they wos in a trance,
While the bloke 'oo is conductin' seems to 'ave St Vitus Dance;
'Arf-time they ups and takes a break wiv Fortnum & Mason 'ampers,
An' 'as a nosh-up on the grass: cold chicken, chocs an' champers.

Oh it's Cozy Fanny Tooty, *'oo-ever she might be,*
But it's all Sweet Fanny Adams to the likes of you an' me.

The stars is mostly Eyties (they know wot it's all abaht),
The ladies 'ave 'uge bosoms, as big as all get-aht,
Wot wiv kissin', shootin' an' stabbin', them operas is 'ot stuff,
An' you need an aht-size bosom so you don't run short o' puff.

As fer Cozy Fanny Tooty *an' all that lah-di-dah,*
Sez Tommy, they can stick the 'ole thing up their repertwhar.

STANLEY J. SHARPLESS

Sydney Opera House

(With apologies to Joyce Grenfell)

Our cultured friends down under decided one fine day
They'd like to have an opera house, where all the best could play.
They wanted something very grand,
And quite spectacular,
So set a competition, with entries near and far.

An architect named Utzorn, from Denmark's seabound land
Put in a very strange design. Though not quite as he planned
The building now, from stern to prow
Stands proud above the sea,
Where opera is floated
(And most of it in key).

As stately as a galleon upon the Sydney shore
This flagship of grand opera stands firmly to the fore.
Its billowed roofs stand plump and tall
As if blown from the sea
(Or maybe they are filled with air from vocal buoyancy!)

Beneath its sails the able crews amuse the guests on board,
With vocal waves and blasts of wind they could not be ignored.
Though many a whine on its design
Has passed through Aussie lips,
It brings more crowds to Sydney
Than all those prison ships.

KATIE MALLETT

Let's Fake An Opera

Let's Fake An Opera

*I look upon opera as a magic scene contrived to please the
eyes and ears at the expense of the understanding.*

Lord Chesterfield

Cutting from The Sun.

SLAPSTICK TO SLAUGHTER
(Clown Turns Double Killer)

FROM ROGER LIONHORSE IN NAPLES

A STAGE farce exploded into a sensational, bloody double
murder horror last night as an ageing, golden-voiced, jealousy-
maddened, white-faced, red-mouthed, motley-clad clown went on
a crazed rampage with a gleaming, ten-inch-bladed knife, slaying
his young, darkly attractive, slim (36–24–36) clownette wife and
her village Romeo lover before a devastated audience of simple
country folk who only seconds before had been laughing at the
slapstick buffoonery on stage.

The carnage that shook the sleepy picture-postcard mountain
village of Montalto was triggered when maestro mountebank
Canio, 50, and his wife Nedda, 28, were playing the roles of
deceived husband *Pagliacco* and unfaithful spouse Colombina in a
golden-oldie comedy. Canio knew the situation was for real and
demanded the name of her lover. When she refused to tell, he
plunged the knife into her. Bonking bumpkin Silvio, mid-twentyish,
rushed to her side and suffered the same fate.

Canio – Mister Showbiz of the Calabrian circuit – was still the
complete pro. He told screaming onlookers: 'That's your lot.' No
ticket money was refunded. A box-office spokesman said: 'They
should be so lucky. It was two shows for the price of one. Bags of
realism too.'

PETER VEALE

The Telefication of the Poet's Cranium

A Videopera

Personification: Vaig Paine, librettist (retired Martian)
Nudgall Frogsporne, composer (current)
Storis Justaknak, author of the *rambella*
from which the ?plot is taken; also takes
part in the opera as Wire-
Crosser/Electrificator.
Seryous, a Poet
Ganasha, his Sister
The Festerings, a Family
Anna Arid, a Governess
Trashka, a Prostitute
and others.

Specification: The ?plot can best be described as
complicated, and we will not attempt to
summarize it, merely remark that the
characters revolve (literally, see
Technification, below) round a Poet (Seryous)
and his relations with his sister, the
household in which he is a tutor, the
Governess, a Prostitute, and Trains.
Revolving round them is the *Crushun
Revolution,* symbolized by the sound of
Zooms in the background. More accessible
than the actual ?plot are the following
aspects of the opera:

(1) *Metrification:* The modest Martian's coming out
With rhyme and pararhyme,
But can we tell what it's about,
Or do we give a dime?
Sometimes he haunts his former scene
And babbles of a time-machine;

Into free verse
He dives;
Then singles
Out jingles
To mingle with his looser style
(I hope by now you've got the feel).

(2) *Technification:* The walls and windows slide about
And catch unlucky singers out;
They grasp the animated wall
Which turns and clips them on the tail;
One moment on the telephone,
The next in bed or in a train
(The Poet's jaw, when this has stopped,
Seems to be permanently dropped).

(3) *Sexification:* The Governess (a widow) slaps
The Poet's face at last,
So as the custom is with chaps,
He seeks another, fast.
Her golden heart is on display
Nor should the critic scoff –
Though it's a shock to hear her say:
'Let's get your trousers off.'
Back to the Governess he goes,
Who seems prepared to wed,
Then finds him in creative throes
So steals away instead.
To round things off, an Epilogue's
Appended ere they quit,
When, dressed in military togs,
She hands the frozen mitt . . .

(4) *Projectification:* But keeps an album full of shots
(Did these appear before,
Like phantoms in unlikely spots
Six feet above the floor?)
Incriminating stuff, it seems,
Which, as the opera ends,

215

Disintegrates like idle dreams
Or tickets when the engine steams,
Or poets' manuscripts in reams,
Or all the paper that in streams
　　　Throughout the work descends . . .

(5) *Identification:* And if this means that it's a waste
　　　　　　Of time to sit and write,
　　　　For once the moral's to my taste;
　　　　　　I've lost my appetite.
　　　　Unnerved, I cast my pen aside
　　　　And wait to be electrified.

MARY HOLTBY

The DIY Opera Kit

Throw another baby on the bonfire,
Fish another pearl out of the deep,
Roast an erring Don until he's on fire,
So Violetta gets her beauty sleep,

Filch a tune or two from Cimarosa,
Shakespeare's a good hunting ground for plots;
Anything by Wagner's comatoser,
Let Ariadne sun-bathe 'til she rots.

Anything from *Boris* clears a full house,
Bulls and fighters, though, both go down well;
If you're stuck then *Arabella* (R. Strauss)
Has jollier tunes than most, save *William Tell*.

Barter a few brides; scour Gluck and Bizet,
Inveigle Hugh the Drover, if it's properer.
But always keep it short and *civilisé*;
Originality has no place in opera.

D. A. PRINCE

A Social Report

Lucia (Also known as 'Mimi')

Report of DHSS Surveillance Officer on Supplementary Benefit claimant 'Mimi'.

A The claimant has not disclosed to the Department that she is living with a man and is therefore, under the regulations, presumed to be supported by him (though a chat with the landlord revealed that the claimant's cohabitee, like all the other roomers in the tenement, was months behind with the rent).

B The claimant alleges that she is a victim of tuberculosis (as a result of working overlong hours in poorly ventilated premises in the rag trade). It is well known that the disease in question was totally eradicated long ago from society; and her claim to be suffering from it is inconsistent, moreover, with the extraordinary and patently healthy lung-power manifested by the incessant singing with which she floods not merely her own apartment but the whole block. (During one of her not infrequent rows with her live-in lover, my audiometer registered a maximum reading of 137 decibels – and this at a distance of at least forty feet from her closed but cracked windows.)

C On the strength of the information contained in the foregoing paragraphs, I recommend that the claimant's Supplementary Benefit be suspended forthwith; and that her case be carefully assessed with a view to her possible prosecution on the grounds of non-disclosure and palpable mendacity.

MARTIN FAGG

Noye's Fludde

A Traumatic Opera

The choir of St Benjamin-on-the-Estate is taking a break when the Voice of the Vicar is heard addressing them. He has had an idea.

> VOICE OF VICAR: I, Smith, that all this churche have
> wrought,
> Choir and bande, and all from nought,
> I have, my people, been out and bought
> Of Noye's Fludde the score.
>
> Therefore, choir, my people free,
> That singë loud when I bid thee,
> All gather round and stand by me
> For to put on a showe . . .

Members of St Benjamin's come forward to offer their skills. The Vicar is well pleased.

> MR SEM: I have a bugle wonder keen,
> To blowë well, as may be seen,
> A better sounden, as I ween,[1]
> Is not in all this town.
>
> MR HAM: And I can bashe right well this tinne
> And with a drumsticke knocke it in
> So I can add unto the dinne
> And I am ready bowne[2] . . .

Rehearsals begin. All manner of musicians are seen approaching St Benjamin's in a great procession. Mr Sem hurries to tell the Vicar.

> MR SEM: Sire, here are stringës, he and she,
> Organ playing merrily,
> Singers singën, you may see,
> Tapping rhythm with their feet.

[1] think
[2] prepared

MR HAM: And here are cellos, cymbals, too,
Cuppës hangen up also,
Recorders, handbelles, piano,
Bringen sandwiches to eat . . .

There are problems with the set and rehearsals begin to founder. The Vicar wishes to use the children of St Benjamin's C. of E. Mixed Primary and the band objects. A great storm is about to break.

VOICE OF VICAR: This showe that I made I will destroye!
Musicians all, that were my joye,
Bande and choir, both man and boye,
So sore it grievës me!

Choir, bande, attend my rime,
They who shoulde act can ne keepe time,
And they who are singers can ne mime,
And the bande stoppes for their tea!

However, tickets have been sold so compromises are reached and the storm passes. The show goes on and, as the last parishioner leaves St Benjamin's, the Vicar addresses his cast.

VOICE OF VICAR: Here I behet thee a heste[3]
That mightie bande and choir bleste,
Ne more will I call peste
That did presente this scene!

My blessing nowe I give thee here.
That ilkë blessing shall appeare
As token for thee, yeare to yeare,
In our Parishe Magazine!

N. J. WARBUTON

---

[3] make you a promise

Parsi fal Tutte

UNKNOWN OPERA DISCOVERED IN SHOEBOX

Music authorities in Munich have announced the find of the decade, an opera score in manuscript, discovered in a shoebox among the personal effects of 'Mad' King Ludwig II of Bavaria. The box has apparently lain undisturbed for a century. The composer was Richard von Mozart, about whom little is known. Ludwig evidently commissioned the work, which was never performed, possibly owing to staging difficulties. The plot of the opera, which was provisionally titled *Parsi fal Tutte*, is as follows.

Act I Count Amoroso's palace in Tuscany. The Count has fallen in love with his wife's maid Tartina, who is in love with Felicio, the Count's manservant (who seems to have figured in an earlier work, *The Barber of Dusseldorf*). Felicio, who himself is secretly in love with the Countess, tells her of the Count's *amours*. She persuades the page Serafino (who is in love with her also) to exchange clothes with her so that she can observe the Count. Amoroso, however, has already changed clothes with Felicio to gain access to Tartina. They all hide. At this point a mysterious stranger enters, clad in pure white. He is Grünasgras, and explains that he is doomed to wander the Earth in pursuit of a mystical sacred chalice. The Countess, who immediately falls in love with him, tries to persuade him to stay, suggesting that they change clothes. Grünasgras hesitates, but the giant Gruffbögger enters, summoning him to resume his eternal quest, and they exit together. The incident seems to put a damper on things at the palace.

Act II A forest glade. By a blasted oak, Grünasgras laments his fate. Then he remembers the magic jewel on the hilt of his sword Käsemesser. He rubs it, and the dwarf Maverich appears from the tree trunk. Maverich, who is a servant of the Dark Forces, offers to give Grünasgras an enchanted potion in return for his immortal soul. Grünasgras agrees. Voices are heard and they hide. The Count's party now enters, all wearing their own clothes. Felicio lays a picnic while the others flirt, hide behind trees, sing quartets etc. As the revels mount, Grünasgras slips the potion into the Count's champagne, which Felicio also samples surreptitiously.

Act III The palace. The potion has taken effect. The Count repents of his licentious life and declares his resolve to journey in search of the Sacred Spear of the Nurburgrings. The Countess at first takes this as an excuse for him to go philandering, but Felicio too declares his desire to put all frivolity behind him and pursue the mystic quest with his master. Gruffbögger now appears in a clap of thunder and summons the Pomaidens to transport the Count and Felicio to the ethereal regions to begin their voyage. The Pomaidens arise from the subterranean depths riding on giant porpoises, which are transformed into flying white horses and disappear into the sky with the Count and Felicio.

Grünasgras, unburdened of his mission, now falls in love with Tartina, who herself falls in love with Maverich. Tartina exchanges clothes with Serafino and conceals herself in an arbour. Meanwhile Maverich, disguised as a simple peasant girl . . .

(The final pages of the M S are faded beyond restoration.)

NOEL PETTY

Aida

AIDA'S TOMB
(*After Philip Larkin*)

This was Aida's tomb. She's walled
Up there with Rameses. At least she knows
The when of death, whatever god it's called
In ancient Egypt. The story (well-known) shows

A simple slave (Aida – sop.) who's got
Her hero in her father's captor: sad.
Her rival, one Amneris, sets the plot
To ditch her. Women aren't all bad.

But opera, unlike jazz, brings out the worst.
Verdi or Mozart, pretty much the same.
In love one woman has to come in first;
But this time no one wins the sexual game.

Some blame the priests, grabbing the martial glory,
Some Rameses, who saved Aida's dad;
It's got the trappings of a decent story —
Power and sex, the things I've never had.

But if the final curtains, patched and frayed,
The sweating singers and the shabby props,
Bring us near understanding love's charade
Or push back death behind the third-rate props,

And make more bearable our own near ending,
Minus, of course, Grand March, and 'our 'ero
Noble in death', I shiver, apprehending
The last unanswered question. I don't know.

D. A. PRINCE

Epilogue

Sleep is an excellent way of listening to opera.

James Stephens

An Opera-lover's Nightmare

(*After W. S. Gilbert*)

When you're lying awake with a dismal headache, having just seen
   Tristan and Isolde,

You're sorry for both, and you'd swear upon oath that you're feeling
   some twenty years older,

As you toss in your bed there's a tune in your head that is practically
   driving you dotty,

But you cannot recall where it comes from at all, or who sang it –
   perhaps Pavarotti

In *Manon Lescaut* or *Les Hugenots* – or maybe in *Dreigroschenoper*,

You eventually settle for *Hansel and Gretel*, it certainly was a show-
   stopper.

Next you dream that The Garden has lost its façade an' appears now
   extremely unsightly,

Lloyd Webber's the boss and you're terribly cross for he's staging *The
   Phantom* twice nightly,

Then you're in the Crush Bar with a world-famous star when,
   unhappily, Nature calls,

So you fight your way through to the Gentleman's loo, but find
   yourself back in the stalls;

A rum sort of show, it's almost as though the Marx Bros had got up a
   gala,

And you're suddenly switched, bewildered, bewitched, to a seat in the
   gods at La Scala,

Where a man with a baton, who's still got his hat on, is conducting an
   overture madly,

And Dame Nellie Melba, who's flown in from Elba, sings *Tosca*,
   surprisingly badly;

There's *Lucia di Lammermoor*, looking quite pale and dour, (funny, this
   isn't her opera),

Her legs are too skinny – she's wearing a mini – a kilt would have
   really been properer,

And what is still queerer, it's 5,000 lire to hire some cheap opera
    glasses;
Now they're playing *Wozzeck*, you've a crick in your neck, and you
    marvel how slowly time passes.
Strauss's *Die Fledermaus* really brings down the house, turns it to
    brick-dust and rubble,
But a magical toot from Mozart's *Magic Flute* restores it without any
    trouble.
Der Fliegende Holländer's next on the agenda, you want to step out for a
    gin,
Wagner for sure is a humourless bore, and you can't think what made
    *Lohen*GRIN.
Good heavens, there's Callas, a guest star in *Dallas*, she's certainly
    widening her scope,
Grand opera's swell, but she says, truth to tell, it's more fun to appear
    in a Soap;
Menotti's *The Medium* inspires you with tedium, Offenbach's worse
    than his bite,
Porgy and Bess – or good old G & S – would be more to your liking
    tonight.
They say the Savoy's a sell-out with *Tannhäuser*, and then you must see
    Peter Grimes,
It's being broadcast with an all-female cast, Mrs Thatcher has seen it
    six times.
You find IBM now sponsors *Bohème*, and elsewhere it's just the same
    story,
Saatchi and Saatchi fund *I Pagliacci* – and, of course, *Il TrovaTory*.
At a Glyndebourne *al fresco* (co-sponsored by Tesco) you run up
    against Michael Tippett,
He invites you to sing in the next season's *Ring*, but you wisely
    determine to skip it;
Then someone you know says that you ought to go to see *Lady
    Macbeth of* (where?) *Mtsensk*,
But the nightmare is past and you wake up at last, and you say very
    firmly, 'NO THENSK!'

STANLEY J. SHARPLESS

INDEX OF AUTHORS

INDEX OF ENCAPSULATED OPERA PLOTS

INDEX OF OTHER VERSE
AND PROSE

Titles of operas in italics   (C) Clerihew   (L) Limerick